The Insightful Parent

Helping Parents Heal so Kids Don't Have to Hurt

by Amanda E. Corbin LCSW

Janelle —
Thank you for your
support! May God
bless you + your
journey!

Amanda

ISBN-13: 978-1975830175
ISBN-10: 1975830172

Editor: Janis M. Whipple
Formatting & layout: www.bookclaw.com

Table of Contents

DEDICATION

First and foremost, thank you, God, for giving me the desire to make a God-difference in this world.

To my near and dear husband of nearly two decades, who encourages, loves, and laughs with me.

To my children, who push me daily to be a better mother and human being.

To my mother, who taught me that time with my kids is so much more important than a clean sink.

To my father, whose support and encouragement have granted me the power to live with passion.

Finally, to my writing coach and editor, who gently encouraged me to start fresh and complete the task with passion.

INTRODUCTION

Have you ever taken a road trip? When I was young, my dad was big on trips—not just the destination but also the journey along the way. He is not a direct-drive kind of guy, perhaps because when he was growing up there were fewer interstates. Or maybe he intentionally chose the side roads to stay out of traffic. Or he discovered local roads to enjoy the small-town fare and people. Whatever the reasons, we were a family of seven in a full-sized Suburban and always took the scenic route. Of all the explanations I can find, I think it came down to one. My dad took us on the scenic route for the experience. He took us on the scenic route because the destination is not what counts as much as the journey.

While I didn't believe it then, I now can appreciate the memories made on those trips. It is fun to watch traditions, like scenic adventures, carry into the next generation. Just this year, I took a trip with my dad and my two children. We have family only a state away that we traditionally visit once or twice a year. We always drive for the financial benefits, so this time was no different. As any parent knows, a trip with children automatically adds thirty minutes to every hour scheduled on the road. With that in mind, I knew our drive would take some time. Potty breaks. Time to get the wiggles out. Snacks and meals. The journey there was fairly uneventful, and we took the interstate most of the way because we were so excited to see our cousins. We had the destination in mind.

When the family visit was over it was time to drive home. The journey back will forever stick in our memories. As I drove along Interstate 10, I was in mom mode—a bit more destination-driven than journey-oriented. My desire was to get home and get home fast. However, my children were hungry and eventually we all needed a break. I was reluctant to get off at an exit with no restaurant signs posted on the off ramp. Looking back, I can laugh, but in the moment I was annoyed. My dad was in the front seat, children in the back as we decided to exit. As we drove along a little country road, looking for a place to stop, I felt I had been time-warped back to the early twentieth century and landed on Route 66. We finally happened upon a tiny town where a railroad crossing was the only traffic light. We found a small diner across from an auto-repair shop. I think the server may have been answering phones for the mechanic between taking orders and serving food. The diner had ten tables, with red-and-white checkered tablecloths, and concrete floors. The kids saw a sign for hand-scooped ice cream and knew if they behaved, ice cream would polish off the meal. I ordered a salad and unsweetened tea. My dad ordered "the special"—blackened fish with hushpuppies and sides.

Dad is a spicy food kind of guy. The spicier the meal, the more he enjoys it. He let the server know he likes things spicy and she definitely made note of it. When the food was served, we began to eat. I knew something was awry when he looked at me and said, through watery eyes and red cheeks, "Amanda, you should try the fish." Hmmm, I was reluctant for two reasons. One, my tolerance for spicy food is below a zero. Two, my tolerance for spicy food is below a zero. Against all my better judgment, I tried it. After all, I had tea and hushpuppies and I was getting ice cream. I thought, *I can recover*. I tried a bite and within seconds my mouth was on fire, nose was running, and face was red. I was laughing more than I was crying because it was silly and nearly impossible how a tiny bite, and I mean tiny, could be so spicy.

By this time, we were all laughing around the table, amazed at how a diner so small, from a spot in the road not even on the map, could have created a dish with so much flavor. Thankfully we were mostly alone in the diner, so the scene we were making had little audience.

Then, my daughter decided to try the fish. I knew her tolerance for spicy was higher than mine but I didn't think it matched my father's. She tried a bite. Nothing. She kept chewing. Nothing. The girl was not fazed by this hell-fired blackened fish. We laughed even more and were flabbergasted that a ten-year-old could tolerate a spicy dish that brought a sixty-year-old, spicy-food champion to tears.

We finished our meal, thanked the cook, got our ice cream, and continued our journey home. Our detour was definitely memorable. I'm glad I decided to ignore my destination-driven mom-mode and take the road less traveled. I can honestly say I appreciate the memory more now than I did the experience at the time, but thankfully I listened to my heart more than my impulse and got off the interstate.

If we hadn't stopped, would we have the memory and laughs to cherish from that day? If I had grumbled throughout the meal, would anyone have had a good experience? If we decided to stay on the interstate, how much of life would we have missed that day? We miss too much of life when we stay focused on the most direct route.

As parents, sometimes our desire to be destination-driven with our children can get in the way of enjoying the parenting journey. And sometimes in the process, we don't realize that our own past journey gets in the way of being an effective parent in the present. We must take a deeper look into our lives to gain the insights needed to heal in our own broken places so our children have a healthy journey on the way to their destinations.

PART 1

FOUNDATION

Before we begin to look at how to become a more insightful parent, some ground rules will help set the foundation for self-evaluation. The process of digging into our past and perhaps the pain and brokenness that may not be healed from it, can be painful in itself. However, it is necessary in order to heal and create the best possible environment for our children to grow into insightful people themselves. Our own healing has positive benefits for them, so it's worth the difficult process we must experience.

In order to discuss healing, let's look first at some foundational knowledge that will help us through the journey to wholeness and insight.

Chapter 1

Journey

Just like my desire to get home quickly on our family trip, society tends to be an interstate culture. We desire to go where we need to go, do what we need to do, and return in the most efficient means necessary. Society is inundated with smart phones. We are rarely without this access to email, texting, the Internet, and the ability to call or FaceTime anyone anywhere in the world at any time. We don't have to wait for anything anymore. We have become a fast-paced culture, conditioned to go, go, go, move, move, move, and we think this is best. We believe the more we do, accomplish, and achieve, the happier we will be. Wrong. All this just makes us more exhausted.

Happiness is not found in objects or events. Happiness is found within, and we can only access that part of us when we are deeply rooted in appreciating life. It is difficult to appreciate something today if we are focused on the regrets of yesterday or anxieties of tomorrow. The first thing that needs to change to begin appreciating the journey of life is your intention, your focus. Commitments like schedules, classes, and dinners might all remain in place, but when you begin to live intentionally, you will learn to appreciate them. It is not about how much or how little we are doing but whether we are intentional in what we say and do, paying attention to life as we live it. This is how we fulfill the goal of viewing life as a journey.

Appreciate the Present

Cell phones, schedules, and dreams can be assets to helping us appreciate life. But they can also be a hindrance if we are not careful. I have a cell phone, I like schedules, and I like achieving goals. These are not great or evil in themselves. The meaning we place on them gives them their value. All these things are tools to help us in life. We are made to be present, mindful beings, and these tools all add to our ability to be present in the moment. However, we must take caution when they become a distraction. If I had been checking emails while I was at lunch on my trip with the family, I would have missed the experience.

I believe we all wear multiple hats, but research has proven we do not multitask. We switch from one task to another at quick speeds and in short intervals. If I was switching from work mode to play mode at the diner that day, I would have missed the emotional connection with my dad and kids.

Memories are made and solidified when an emotion is simultaneously experienced with an event. Then a meaning is assigned to the memory, making it a core memory.

Great memories and relationships are not built on efficient routes and schedules. If we strive for efficiency, we make the most direct plan, minimizing time, money, and distractions. But we hinder relationships in the process. Building relationships takes time. Not that relationships can't be maintained in efficiency, but they are seldom nurtured or initiated when someone is focused solely on results. Because of this, if a person is too task-oriented, they can have difficulty maintaining strong relationships. To appreciate life and relationships, we must be willing to stop, breathe, and enjoy being present.

You are reading this book because you already know the value of investing time in something. You know the value of spending time cuddling on the couch with your child. You know the value of receiving a card in the mail from someone special. When you think about the memories that hold value to you, what are they about? Food? Family? Friendships? Faith?

What Has Value to You?

Value is defined as something of worth or importance. You and I may value things differently. Positive or negative, whatever we value dictates our lives. I have two dear friends, Becky and Paige, who immensely value the journey of life. I call them collectors of friends, because they seldom meet a stranger and everyone is a friend. Becky and Paige believe they can learn something from everyone. Their days are filled with plans, activities, gatherings, books, and adventure. They are collectors of life's beauty and experiences. They learn from the horror in life, celebrate the awesomeness, and hold tight in between. They have learned the value of life through sacrifice and hardship. They desire to share in life's beauty with others, and I admire their passion for pursuing joy. Along with valuing the journey, I have seen through them that knowledge and insight are found within the journey. As you learn more, you become aware that insight is not taught or told, but rather experienced and internally gained. Insight is like a GPS for life; when we are off course, if we listen to insight, it recalculates our journey to keep us on the right path.

I know this is easier said than done. I know there is a critical voice in your head thinking this is easier for me to type than for you to read. Well, nothing I write here is false, arrogant, or without serious trial and error on my own part. By nature, I am a task-oriented person. By grace, I am a people person. Still today, when given a job or a task, my impulse is to drive full speed toward achieving the goal. Without grace, my life would look like a construction site. I would use a bulldozer to flatten any obstacles, reach my goal, and feel thrilled for a moment. But when I look behind me and see the destruction this causes, I know I can't handle life this way. I constantly need grace to make the right choices and prioritize the value of my relationships. So, I have learned it is the journey that counts.

Parenthood is a task, and certainly not easy. As parents, we tend to focus on the destination. We want to get our children into adulthood. We hope they make it there without too many bumps, bruises, or scars, and we especially hope we aren't the creator of too many scars. But as soon as parenthood begins, we learn the experience isn't the task we thought it would be. We learn that bumps, bruises, and scars are inevitable. And we hurt for our children when they hurt. We know that the old childhood rhyme "Sticks and stones may break my bones, but words will never hurt me" is entirely untrue. The deepest scars happen when someone speaks hurtful words to our children or us. The journey of parenthood is to help our children as much as we can and harm them the least. Parenthood takes relationships. It takes love. It takes every fiber of your being sometimes to keep it together. It also takes healing from the bumps, bruises, and scars in your own past. The journey isn't easy but it is worth it, because our children will pursue life often in the same manner we allowed them to explore life. Our journey, the appreciation we show for life, and the healing we achieve will help our kids develop their own journey and values.

High-Speed Parenting

Imagine what parenthood would look like if we sped through it at high speed. Living so rapidly as if life was an interstate. Passing all major cities and states to reach the end of the journey. There are many errors in this thinking. First, the journey and role of parenting is never over; it just changes. While the relationship is often more mature, a parent's heart for their adult children still longs for their safety and success. Once a parent, always a parent. It is important to know, the role of parent is not necessarily tied to DNA or biology, and we will cover this later.

Another flaw in the interstate lifestyle logic is the plethora of life events missed at high speeds between the exits. Life is about these events, these pauses, pit stops, and stoplights that give us the opportunity to make deep connections to the ones we love. The interstate is necessary, but remember to get off to fuel up, eat, and stretch your legs. It is a good thing to keep the goal in sight, but don't ignore the stops along the way.

A Delicate Balance

All this talk about the journey and not the destination may seem like overkill, but realistically, in life most of us are on the journey because we know there is a destination ahead. My encouragement is to not be so consumed with the destination but allow it to shape and guide your journey.

Despite this plug for being free-spirited and freethinking, I am actually a semi structured person. Research shows that structure brings comfort and security in our lives. I believe it does. In celebrating the journey, we can still have structure, but we must exhibit heartfelt sound judgment and value in the things we put on our schedule. We want our children to be healthy, so we sign them up for sports. We want our children to value family and relationships, so we attend family events. These things are good, but when we place value more in the fulfillment of the task rather than the benefit to our children, and ourselves we are misguided.

Before you sign up for another season or commit to another event, ask yourself, "Do my kids enjoy the soccer games?" "Is family dinner at the grandparents' house every Sunday what is best for my family?" These are questions I've learned to ask myself. The journey is about balance. Knowing what you and your children need and balancing it with confident parenting keeps you sane. Learn to discover the balance for you and your family by making wise choices in how you structure your lives and how much you celebrate and enjoy what you do. Your ability to enjoy and balance life on the journey will teach your children how to process and problem-solve as adults.

I believe life must be appreciated. Let me correct that: I *learned* that life must be appreciated. If it isn't, it will be wasted by you and a waste for others. A few years back I took a full-time job as a manager at a large nonprofit. This was my first full-time job since before having children. I took the job for two reasons: the money and the desire to make better use of the master's degree I'd earned. The job consumed me. Within two months, I was working sixty-plus hours a week dealing with audits, grants, and chronically ill individuals. I was spent. I had nothing left when I went home. My children got the last of me, my husband got pieces of me, and I had nothing left for me. I was not appreciating life. I scaled back at work, asked for a demotion to help balance things, and waited for God to open a door that let me walk out. I knew I was done. I knew I wanted more from life. I knew there had to be more from life. Within six months of the demotion, my husband was offered a job, dollar for dollar exactly what I was making. That was confirmation enough for me. I gave notice and resigned. The first three weeks I was home, I began to appreciate life. I wanted to be healthy for myself.

We must want to be better for ourselves, not just our children. You are too important to not play a valuable part in your own life. Our children will do what we do, not what we say. If I live a zealous, ambitious, heartfelt life, my children will see that. If I give up, forfeit the fight, and live by heartache, my children will see that.

I decided to be intentional, learn from past experiences, and never again become who I was at that job. I was amazed at the new perspective I gained about the "small" things. For years I had missed them. I didn't know the name of my daughter's best friend. I didn't know what my son liked in his lunch. I was missing life. The destination had mattered so much, I missed the journey. This wasn't interstate driving; this was high-altitude, long-distance flight. I missed it. Don't miss the little things. Stop. Look. Listen. Pay at least as much attention to your life and your family's life as you do when you want to cross the street.

The Developmental Journey

As a mental health counselor and a mother, I get a double whammy of having a thinker mind. If I don't have someone in front of me that I am helping through a problem, I'm in my own head working through problems. If it sounds exhausting, it is. Yet in the thinking I have found value in trying to simplify things. Knowledge is power, and in the right dose, knowledge can be a stress reducer by helping us simplify the issues in our lives.

Two tools I use to help me breathe as a parent, and that I share with other parents, are Erikson's stages of development and Maslow's hierarchy of needs. Learning these developmental stages and needs helps parents gain general knowledge about what a child's and adult's needs are at certain stages of life, so we can recognize our own physical, emotional, and social needs and, in turn, those of our children. Once you can understand and gauge your own life's journey, you can then transfer that success to recognizing and meeting your children's needs.

Erik Erikson was a psychologist in the 1900s who studied human development. He recognized that at various stages from birth to death, individuals achieve basic stages of life in order to develop corresponding virtues. Fulfilling these stages results in a healthy, independent, well-adjusted adult. If a stage is not achieved, the virtue is not instilled in the person.

The first stage is trust versus mistrust and happens between the ages of birth to two years, and if this stage is successfully achieved, the child will develop hope. Trust is primarily learned through feeding and the primary caregiver. The second stage is autonomy versus shame and doubt. This occurs from ages two to four, and is developed through basic independent skills like play and learning to dress oneself. The virtue to be achieved in this stage is will. The additional stages, virtues, and ages are listed on the chart below.[1]

Stage	Psychosocial Crisis	Basic Virtue	Age
1	Trust vs. mistrust	Hope	Infancy (0 to $1^{1/2}$)
2	Autonomy vs. shame	Will	Early Childhood ($1^{1/2}$ to 3)
3	Initiative vs. guilt	Purpose	Play Age (3 to 5)
4	Industry vs. inferiority	Competency	School Age (5 to 12)
5	Ego identity vs. role confusion	Fidelity	Adolescence (12 to 18)
6	Intimacy vs. isolation	Love	Young Adult (18 to 40)
7	Generativity vs. stagnation	Care	Adulthood (40 to 65)
8	Ego integrity vs. despair	Wisdom	Maturity (65+)

If we study Erikson's work, it is undeniable that success is found in attaining the virtues along the journey. Life is a process and series of little events, but every little event has purpose in developing a healthy person. Look at the virtues described in the various stages and think of how a child or adult learns it. We learn through experience. We retain and truly find our identity not by what is told to us but by what we experience in life. Thus, learning to recognize when negative experiences may have shaped an unhealthy result is the first step in healing and moving forward on our life's journey.

Erikson's profound work provides a basis for me to identify where my children are in their journeys and what virtue I can help develop in them at each stage. The stages also give me an opportunity to reflect on my life, and whether I believe I have appropriately developed the earlier virtues. Just like the

GPS in our car, it is never too late to recalculate on our journey. Any virtue can be learned at any time. It is never too late to develop a virtue and experience the fullness of it in your life. This chart is not law, but simply a guideline to help understand how life experiences are building blocks for adulthood. Pay more attention to the conflict and virtues of each stage and less attention to the age.

Virtues are internal attributes that are developed and achieved, and they create a framework for how we live life. Needs, at their basic level, are external, and must be provided by others, starting when we are young. Psychologist Abraham Maslow developed a theory focusing on needs of individuals. He determined that all individuals progress through a series of needs in life, each built upon the previous need, like a pyramid. Lower needs must be met before moving up to higher ones. All pyramids require a wide foundation to build on. Maslow determined that the foundation of all needs is our basic physiological needs. For inner needs of love and belonging to be met or even addressed, basic physiological and safety needs must be fulfilled.[2]

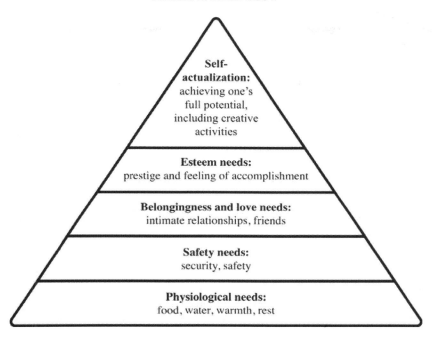

As you reflect on Maslow's pyramid, you may feel comfort or conflict. It will depend on your own experience and the experience you are able to provide for your child. Remember that being able to provide the basic needs for your child goes a long way. Focusing on basic needs and then progressing to psychological needs will ensure a strong foundation for your children. Maslow appropriately ordered it in three categories: basic needs, psychological needs, and self-fulfillment, in sequential order. A parent's greatest desire is to have healthy kids, and Maslow gives a framework for meeting your child's basic needs.

Erikson and Maslow help construct the roadmap for the journey that many parents feel blind walking. They help us see the path by educating us about what we need. While knowledge is important and can help our children and us, we can't let it paralyze us or make us feel like a failure. Do not use these tools like grading scales. Healthy parenting is a balance of knowledge and faith.

We were not made to live in fear. Fear is paralyzing and destructive. I believe the current generation of parents of young children is high on the spectrum of fear and we live more through paranoia than faith. Fear of not being able to protect our children can cause us to homeschool, isolate, and coddle our children. Independently, homeschooling can provide wonderful experiences for our children, but fear-based decisions to avoid the alternative is no way to parent or live. Fear of our children getting germs leads us to stay withdrawn and our children suffer with poor social skills or lack deep relationships. We all need to have a healthy awareness of the world around us, but fear should not be the basis for our parenting methods. Life is meant to be enjoyed, and fear and feelings of failure will keep us from enjoying it.

Dealing with Expectations

Life comes with no road map and often only enough light for the step we are on. On this journey, we do not always know what lies ahead. Sometimes it is difficult to move beyond what lies behind. But if we live from the past, we will never open the present, and the future will be destroyed before it starts. Whether we choose to heal or remain hurt from the past will undoubtedly affect our lives, our families, and our relationships.

Whether our past left us healthy or harmed, we traverse through life with expectations, hopes, and desires. If healthy, we may expect to live a long, healthy life. We expect we will be safe in life. We expect to be financially stable as adults. Conversely, if harmed by our past, we might expect spouses will cheat, children will rebel, and parents will abandon us. Expectations can be realistic or unrealistic. The negative experiences are the ones that sting. They hurt. We feel betrayed, unloved, disrespected. Our expectations shape how we live and view life. For better or worse, if we do not recognize the influence expectations have on our lives, decisions, and relationships, they can destroy everything we value. So, we must stay grounded and begin to self-reflect on what we expect from our children, family, coworkers, friends, and ourselves.

Our expectations have been created by our own experiences. When we are young, expectations can be ideal and innocent. But when something bad happens, expectations can be filled with fear, sadness, loss, or regret. One analogy I use to acknowledge our past experiences and the proper place negative experiences have in our life is paint cans. Paint is a fascinating thing. It comes in so many colors, textures, and types. It can be oil-based, latex-based, tempera, or acrylic. Its colors exceed the hues in the rainbow. Paint is so powerful a substance, its ability to permanently alter anything it comes in contact with is its greatest strength and weakness alike. When you go to a paint store, how is the paint stored? In heavy metal cans that both preserve the paint and protect the objects in its vicinity from being touched. Paint needs to be contained until the artist or painter decides it's time to use it.

Paint is best used individually. Unless a painter is skilled, just mixing two colors from two cans with no rhyme or reason usually results in a muddy, mint-brown hue. Few things look good with a muddy, mint-brown hue. You don't generally mix paint colors. When you want white, you use white. When you want blue, you use blue. When you want black, you use black. Colors are used independently and then layered on a surface with skill and well-acquired talent. When a painter is not using the paint, he closes the lid and places it on the shelf until it is needed again.

Imagine a large display of shelves in front of you, about four rows tall and several feet wide. Each shelf contains a number of gallon paint cans, with space between the cans. Now, imagine these cans are not full of paint. They are full of your life experiences—the difficult experiences that need to be contained. When you imagine all these experiences, you may feel as if you've painted your wall a muddy mint-brown. Several paints have run together and made a mess of the things. But the cans can be closed and lids secured, because the difficult experiences are separate issues and need to be addressed as such.

Now, imagine the cans on your shelves and the labels are blank. Each can needs to be labeled. What will you label them? Abuse, abandonment, rejection, death, divorce, pain? As you consider the areas of hurt and difficulty in your life, identify and label the cans one by one. One. By. One. You can do this in your head or on a sheet of paper (see appendix A). This is how we will approach our journey of gaining insights— one topic, one issue, one step at a time. Give yourself permission today to contain your hurt and pain in these cans. As long as we continue to see our present through our past, these experiences still control us. This is why the journey is so significant.

Our expectations and beliefs from the past shape present experiences. If you have experienced some of life's hardest moments, then it takes more work to reach the point of accepting and believing the journey is worth the ride. If you have never experienced the harder things in life, please continue to listen to those who have and offer hope. We can learn from one another regardless of background. The process of reaching the point of seeing life with hope and purpose comes through processing where you have come from and where you are going. I believe wholeheartedly that life is a gift. Even in the wake of hurt, pain, or shame, each day is an opportunity to choose how you will live. I have lived through some of life's hardest moments, and continue to learn the best ways to live out this journey. Welcome to the journey. Trust yourself and trust the process.

Questions to Ponder

1. How would you characterize your parenthood journey up to now? Has it been focused more on the destination or the journey itself?

2. How can you and your family create more balance between the destination and the journey? What would you change about how your family experiences your journey together and how?

3. How have expectations affected the roles you play and others play in your life and family relationships? How

can you adjust these expectations to create a healthier family environment?

4. What did you learn about needs and virtues from Erikson and Maslow? How does this new information bring new understanding about yourself or your family members?

Activity:

Complete the paint can activity in appendix A. How can you better separate the issues represented by your paint cans so that you can have a healthy approach to dealing with them and making positive changes for yourself and your children?

Chapter 2

Insight

As parents, we love to do for our children. We love to give, provide, and encourage. We want our children to know they can have it all in life. We do this through activities, schooling, adventures, and clubs because we believe they provide a sense of identity, confidence, and security for our children. However, we live in a society that values busyness, even when we may not know the purpose behind all the activities that keep our children or us busy. The process of developing insight as a parent means in part that we make decisions about our children's activities intentionally, not because of pressure or the desire to compete with other seemingly "perfect" families. When we get too busy we don't understand the value of balance and rest, and our children learn the same unhealthy lifestyle.

So, what exactly does it mean to gain insight? What is insight? We must delve into our past and examine our motives behind the choices we make for our children.

When Mike was young, he was raised by a single mother and was never involved in activities, as she always struggled just to cover rent. She was a cashier by day and stock person by night. Her time was work and sleep. Mike had to fend for himself, which gave him the work ethic he has today. When Mike was in college he decided his future children would never lack for anything.

Today Mike is a single dad raising his three children on his own. His wife, their mother, passed away three years ago from cancer. As a cardiac surgeon, finances are not a problem for Mike, and all the children's basic needs are met. Each child is involved in at least one afterschool activity every day of the week. Between dance, karate, gymnastics, and church, some would say it is the American Dream. Even before his wife passed, he wanted to be sure his children experienced the "best" in life, that they experienced the adventure of life. Since she passed, his desire has intensified.

Mike doesn't slow down, between midnight pages from the hospital and running his kids to activities after school. He is spent. He has been prescribed sleeping pills to help him wind down at night, but it is not helping. His children see it. His oldest, only ten, prepares dinner every night, and his youngest, five, suffers from separation anxiety at school. While Mike intends to give his children the best, he's missing what matters most: his health, his time, and the children's emotional health.

There is no easy answer to Mike's life. The life he lives now is nothing close to the dreams he had as a boy. It has been changed and impacted by his experience as a child, losing the love of his life, and raising three children as a single father. It is all so much to handle, Mike tends to avoid it. He fills his and his children's time with work, school, and activities, only to be home to sleep. His decisions seem to be made because of his own painful experiences and not out of the strengths and uniqueness of each of his children. While activities are good, they must be balanced with the right intent and healthy outcomes.

Regarding life's struggles, there are two basic types of people: those who address issues (problems) and the type who ignore them. People who address issues are the ones who look at problems and say, "This is unhealthy and should not continue." They believe ignoring it will only prolong the inevitable. They believe *the value in talking about the problem is greater than the pain of ignoring it.* People who ignore problems are the ones who say, "Talking about it would make it worse." They fear talking about it might upset someone and that *the pain of addressing it is greater that the value of resolving it.* What type of person are you?

In Mike's case, we can see why he would avoid the issues. Grief takes time. Healing takes time. And when there are three children to feed and lives to save at the hospital, his personal stuff can wait. But his personal stuff is getting in the way. He avoids the issues because it is painful for him and his children. But even if we avoid the pain, it is still there. Pain and crisis never go away when ignored; they just display themselves in other ways until we resolve them.

Perhaps you're like Mike, in survival mode. While avoiding pain can sometimes provide a temporary relief and give us the energy to deal with immediate family and life needs, the pain will eventually need to be addressed. So where are you in dealing with pain and crisis? Are you inclined to sway one way or the other? How you approach things can vary based on environment, experience, and relationships. You likely have an innate desire to either ignore or address issues. Insight begins with recognizing this about yourself. Neither tendency is right or wrong in itself, but awareness is the first step in growing as a person and a parent.

Personally, I don't like ignoring things. I don't even like beating around the bush. I tend to see problems and directly address them. If there is an elephant in the room, I say we talk about it. Elephants only belong in two places: nature and zoos, and the latter is debatable. But if you leave an elephant in a room long enough, your family and house will smell and feel like a zoo. Ignoring a problem doesn't mean the problem doesn't exist. It just means you are ignoring the problem.

Addressing issues brings healing and positive change. Writing this book has definitely made me take my own advice. Since my first child was born, I've made efforts to examine my childhood experiences before I decide what's best for my daughter and son, so that I base decisions on their welfare, not my own experiences. And I have failed many times. Often, I have to reflect and be sure I'm leading out of love, not fear. When a decision or reaction is out of fear, I apologize and revisit the decision.

You may also have these moments of reflection. You have picked up this book for a reason. Whether out of curiosity, desperation, apathy, or assignment, it is in your hands. So, ask yourself these questions: Do I know what insight is? Do I believe I have insight about things? How does my insight or lack of insight affect my parenting?

What is Insight?

Insight is both a daily practice and a lifelong process. The more we are willing to know and admit about our own selves, the better we can connect and parent our children. There are varying ways to define insight. In its simplest form, it is *in-sight*. The word itself tells you what to do and where to do it. *Look within.* Dictionaries describe it as gaining a deep understanding. Other words used to describe it are *intuition*, *discernment*, and *perception*. For our purposes, I want to consider a broader meaning: *Insight is not the absence of problems or obstacles but rather the awareness of them, recognition of their role in your life, and intentional decision to not let them hinder you in the present or future.* Insight requires awareness, recognition, acceptance, and choice.

As you look within, you will learn to put life events into perspective so they are no longer a hindrance on your journey. In learning to pay more attention to your own internal needs, you will become acutely aware of the needs of others. How? Insight helps you address your own issues so they don't become issues for your loved ones. Then you are free to address the needs of others. While it may seem selfish as a parent to process your own needs first, authentic insight leads to healthy decisions for yourself and others.

While other people and circumstances may contribute, insight is always an internal shift. It must be self-discovered. It must be experienced. Insight is that "ah-ha" moment when experience and understanding collide. Self-discovery is a journey that never ends and uncovers beautiful views along the way. When you grant yourself permission to look within, you begin a process that is painful and ugly at times, but produces a rich, deep love for parts of yourself and others that you otherwise might overlook or even despise. I love insight because it is the first step in the process to a better you. It was the first step in the process to a better me.

Let me give an example. In recent years, I've decided to learn from life's experiences. I'd had enough bad happen that I wanted to learn from it for two reasons: one, to not experience it again myself; two, to help prevent others from experiencing it. Now, my life is not an open book to all people. I pay attention to what parts of my life are relevant to the situation. I choose who, when, and where I share my different stories with different individuals. I share a story of financial hardships with young couples struggling to make ends meet. I share my story of overcoming abuse with survivors who are paralyzed by fear. I listen to the grieving adult trying to choose how to handle the imminent death of their parent and I share my experience being that adult child sitting beside the hospice bed as a family member passed. Life is hard. But when I stumble and fall, when I pick myself back up, I want to know what to look for so I don't fall on the same rock again. I don't believe in failure. The only failure is failing to learn from life's experiences. I believe we can be wrong, and I am wrong often, but I am not a failure as a result. Neither are you.

This may all be new to you and you may feel a bit overwhelmed. All this talk of self-reflection may stir up feelings that are all too familiar and uncomfortable. I'm sorry for the barrage of emotions if they are flowing, but please don't give up. In the next chapter we will learn coping skills that you will be able to use to settle yourself when you become unsettled. If you experience an emotional response, it may tempt you to stop before you go further, but this will not help you or your child. The truth is, life is hard and parenting is no cakewalk. Kids often increase our anxiety. They can trigger our memories, so we need to stop and recognize this when it happens. I want to help you develop awareness—insight—and then move to the point of living in faith not fear. Can you imagine the freedom in saying to yourself, "I'm not comfortable with this but I know that is my experience talking and that my child will be safe"? Or "I don't want my fear to consume my decisions anymore." We want to be great parents, and if we didn't care so much, life wouldn't hurt so much.

Parents, we spend so much time keeping our walls up and trying to keep our act together for sake of our children, we don't take the time to heal so that our walls can come down and we can be healthy for our children. It is time to stop hiding the hurt and allow yourself to heal so you can parent your child better. I want you to love your child because you love yourself. This book is titled *The Insightful Parent*, because it starts with you. I want to help you heal and develop insight so you can read and respond to your own needs. When you read and respond to yourself in healthy ways, you can then read and respond to your children in healthy ways.

I want to encourage you in this journey to focus on the process not the end goal. Right now, decide that the process is okay. Allowing time to heal the pain is okay. Learning more about yourself to help your children is okay. The process may require you to stop and reflect. Please stop in these moments; breathe; reflect on what you are feeling, thinking, and remembering; and write these thoughts in the margins if you want. Use this book as a reference for now and in the future. So much of it will mean different things to you in five and ten years than right now because time changes us and we change with time.

Essential Terms

While there will be numerous topics addressed in this book, I want to focus on a few terms I have seen to be most influential in individuals' lives and will be used regularly in the following chapters.

Parent

You may be a parent and, likely, you had parents. Parents can be the biological individuals who birthed us, but may also be guardians, adoptive parents, or older individuals who dramatically impacted our lives in some way. Allow yourself to assign who plays this role as it applies throughout your life and this book. One of the most fascinating concepts I teach people is that family is not made by blood; family is created by behavior. I have a biological mother and father, who thankfully are wonderful parents and therefore I still call them family. I also have an adoptive mother, who was a spiritual and emotional support to me that filled a deep need at a crucial time in my life. I do not mean to say that you should remove yourself from your family if you feel they haven't met *every* need. I am talking about creating healthy boundaries, allowing the good to remain and either limiting or removing the bad. As you continue this journey, you will process through life and begin to see the good and bad in individuals and reflect on their influence in your life and your influence in theirs.

Parent may identify you as a biological, adoptive, or guardian figure in a child's life. You do not have to be the biological parent to have the opportunity and responsibility of guiding a child into healthy adulthood.

Child

Another concept to be clear about is *child*. You were once a child and you may have children. You may have also been a parent to a child who is no longer under your care. Children are easily influenced. Children are young. They are impressionable and learn by observing and experiencing. They do what we do, not what we say. Children are the hope for the next generation. And we were once the hope for our parents' generation. When you were young, life may have looked different or it may be similar to your children's lives now. Inevitably, when a child grows up, they either repeat or reject the parenting style they received. Every adult was once a child.

All children are not raised with the same family structure or life experiences. Children are shaped and learn to connect with others through their immediate family unit. If the family unit is nontraditional, their experiences will also be nontraditional. You can begin to see how having our needs met as a child, and the way those needs were met, develops who we are as people, and further, as parents. Conversely, we know that not having our needs met or having negative experiences also develops who we are. The foundation of every adult was established through experience and relationships in our childhood.

Crisis

In short, crisis is change—immediate sudden change that we are not in control of. Crisis is difficult for many reasons. Humans do not like what we don't understand. And when something is immediate and sudden, we do not have the chance to understand it. Crisis can be large or small. It can be a child starting at a new school, a family moving across the state, or losing a family member. Crisis stops us in our tracks. It throws us off course and can change our perspective on life. I would describe a crisis as the rock that I trip on and fall flat on my face.

Trauma

Trauma is a crisis that you feel you cannot recover from. While crisis is immediate and not longstanding; trauma is when we can't move forward from the crisis. Trauma is the aftermath of a crisis when we experience long-term emotional or mental change and daily difficulty functioning. Trauma feels paralyzing, and individuals who have experienced trauma feel like they can never again be who they were before. They feel isolated and alone. In my work, for those who have overcome trauma, many will say they don't want to be who they were before the trauma, because they're so much stronger now. If you have experienced the pain of trauma, you can be better and stronger than who you were before. Trauma is such a deep, dark doorway that in the moment, we can't see or believe the sun will come out tomorrow. But the sun will come out tomorrow.

Secondary Trauma

Secondary trauma is when an individual witnesses or hears about an event that affects them so dramatically it alters their view of life. For our generation, the clearest example of an event when everyone can remember where they were and what they were doing was 9/11. Many people lost loved ones and were directly involved in recovery efforts at ground zero. This is a direct relationship to the event and it is primary trauma. For those of us who did not know someone personally affected by 9/11, but we were still changed by 9/11, this is called secondary trauma. September 11, 2001—we remember where we were and what we saw on the news. We remember the shock. We remember feeling helpless and unprepared. We remember feeling violated and angry. We remember hurting for our American family. We became a family who grieved. Airports now feel different. We might have a heightened fear of not feeling safe. Living in fear after an event that was witnessed, or heard about secondhand, is a symptom of secondary trauma.

I tell you about secondary trauma in the context of family and relationships because it demonstrates the impact of any trauma on relationships. After 9/11, for a while it felt like all Americans became family. But then as time went on, many of us went back to our old lives, the American unity faded away, and we all were back in our bubbles. Even then, for some, fear followed us into the bubble, and that is trauma. If you are experiencing fear from trauma, allow the awareness you gain about yourself to replace faith for fear.

Abuse and Neglect

These are the big two. Children and adults are forever changed by these two. It is important to shed light on these issues but not wade too long in these waters. I know already your emotions may be getting stirred if this is part of your life journey. If that is the case, breathe. Breathe. If you have had this experience, you may want to step away for a moment. However, remember you are a survivor and you can do this.

Simply put, abuse is an attack, and neglect is withholding of a need. Children and adults need love, affection, food, shelter, water, and clothing. Children thrive in education and opportunity. Abuse and neglect can come in the form of emotional, mental, physical, sexual, spiritual, or verbal. Parents and adults have to be mindful of the beautiful responsibility we have to train a child in the way they should go. We must tread carefully to tend to children through the eyes of love and not pride or fear. If you have unaddressed or unresolved neglect or abuse in your past, one of two things will happen: you will repeat the cycle or you will parent from a place of hurt and pain. Both responses are a grave injustice to our children. They need love and affection. They need care and concern. You need to be healthy for you and your child(ren).

If you have addressed past abuse or neglect, you may already have the insight and know the value in security and support. Continue your journey of healing and take with you all the tools for healthy living and decision-making.

If you have not experienced abuse or neglect, this is the opportunity to learn more about someone you love. With the rates of abuse being so profound, likely you are aware of someone who experienced it in their life and you can help. The first thing the victim of abuse or neglect needs is security and support.

Loss and Grief

Loss is another crisis in life that can become trauma. Many people have a difficult time with loss and grief. Loss is losing someone or something of value. You may have lost a friendship as a child when you changed schools. You may have lost a parent or pet recently. Grief is the process of reflection and allowing the loss to be of value to you, of honoring the person or thing lost. Loss is a crisis because we can never fully prepare for something to be taken away from us. A person actually being gone is different than thinking about them being gone. The tangible loss takes a person to a traumatic place at times. Grief is the path to acceptance of the crisis or the loss. Grief has several stages: denial, anger, bargaining, depression, and acceptance. Loss is immediate. Grief can take years. Grief is the process of living with the loss and all its aftermath. Most loss is not a singular loss; it has ripple effects for the rest of our lives.

For instance, Sherry was a star tennis player in her college days. She set school and national records and received endorsements from large companies. She was set to train for the Olympics and already had signing deals to play professionally. Sherry's fiancé was also an athlete, a football player at the same college. He had already been drafted to play for the next season. She was well on her way to living the American Dream. One afternoon, Sherry had a car accident after practice that totaled her car. She spent several days in the hospital and suffered permanent damage to her legs and hips. She would never walk again. She would never play tennis again. When she exited the hospital, her dreams exited her life as well. She never again played tennis. She lost the endorsements and her fiancé and dropped out of college. She suffered a loss of both physical and emotional magnitude. The grief was overwhelming and it was years before Sherry was able to move on. When she did, her story of overcoming hardship became an inspiration to young athletes and entrepreneurs.

Grief can be paralyzing if we remain stuck at any point. Grief is a deep healing process that takes us past the brink of darkness. We have to step into the driver's seat again and begin the journey to heal. If you've had a recent loss, you may not be willing to move out of idle right now, but just thinking about moving on is progress. Loss is immediate. Grief can be a lengthy process, but if we remain stuck in grief, we are worlds away from hope, purpose, and new dreams.

Faith

Faith is trust and belief in something. Some sources say it's complete trust and confidence in someone or something. Faith is where we find our strength, and it is important that what we put our faith in can handle it, can be dependable. I stress to individuals the caution we should have when we put faith in a person or a job. I don't want you to have faith in something that does not have a guarantee. Your source of faith needs to be a constant, unchanging source because this is where you draw your strength and identity. If your source of faith fails, you can be broken at your center of identity. Our faith is our core and our basis for identity and purpose. It is a belief system. My faith has been an integral part of gaining insight in my life. I have a confidence in God that has been tested and proven through my years of following him.

Trusting the Process

While we are on the subject of faith, let me tell you a little about this book and the process. I want you to have faith in a few things—yourself, me, the process, and God.

Believe in yourself because you are resilient and strong. Believe in yourself because you have made it this far and will continue to make it. Faith is belief. Believe that you will be able to gain personal insights and learn to listen to those insights and think before you speak or act. And when you mess up. Forgive yourself and seek forgiveness from others.

I ask that you have faith in me because I believe I have the balance of experience and education to help you in this process. I have a bachelors and masters degree in social work and have been working with children and families in community organizations since 2000. I have sat with countless youth and seen the needs of both parent and child. I know that parents need to heal as much as their children do. I have two biological children of my own, and have worked in social services and the foster system for almost two decades, and have hosted exchange students from multiple countries. It is quite an experience to be a mother of biological and "adopted" children. Every child needs to be parented differently. And I may respond to each child differently. Like I said, insight is a journey and I don't always get it right. When I'm wrong and I "react" instead of respond to my children, I go and apologize. When our children learn the art of mercy and forgiveness from us as parents, they will repeat it as adults.

Now, remember I said to have faith in the process? This process will be as fast or slow as you make it. If you go too fast, you will miss it, because change happens over time. You will have both epiphany moments and silent moments. When you have both, stop and revel in it. Applaud yourself for the progress, reflect on how it changes your view of things, and record it somewhere. Journaling is a good thing to start as you read this book. There will be questions throughout, and I will ask you to look back, look ahead, or reflect on your present life and apply what we are talking about.

Begin to use this book as an interactive tool, not to be read front to back and not applied. It is called *The Insightful Parent* for a reason. To develop insight, you must stop, look, and listen. We spend more time learning how to make sure a car is not coming before we cross the street than we do making sure our soul and emotional state is healthy on a regular basis.

Insight is not just awareness in itself; it's also about applying that awareness to our daily choices. When we fail to grow in our insights and rely solely on past experience, we operate with poor insight. The best visual I can think of about poor insight is that we sometimes view life through outdated lenses. For instance, I will ask you to reflect on the past, but I do not want you to stay there. We are not living in the past. This process of gaining insight and healing will take you from old to new, like going from an old TV to a current high-definition, new-technology TV. You wouldn't choose to buy an old-fashioned TV with a poor black-and-white picture to watch a brand-new high-definition movie. In the same way, we don't want to view our present life through old filters. Let the old memories be on the old TV and your present and future on a new TV. It's time to replace the old 1950s TV with a twenty-first-century high-definition screen. The best thing about the past is that it's over.

I want you to trust in God. At least trust me that he got me through my hardest points in life. I can't imagine how I would have gotten through life this far without him. I say that because if you, like me, have experienced pain in this world, how could you trust in a world where you experienced pain, hurt, and loss? I couldn't, so for me, God has been the balance to the unpredictability of this world. Let me start by saying I believe in a God that allows you to ask the hard questions. I believe that the more you learn about yourself the closer you will come to God. I believe every good and perfect gift is from above, and therefore, progress made is progress made toward him. Know that God is with you and waiting for you on this journey. One of the greatest steps I took in my faith was to ask God why. Is there anything you need to ask God why about?

The Ripple Effect

We are visual creatures, and if we can construct an idea and understand it with our mind's eye, the concept sticks better. The whole concept of insight, expectations, and connections can seem like foreign concepts, but a picture is worth a thousand words, so let's paint one. Imagine that we are all in the ocean of life. The ocean is wide and vast, and boats are in sight, but a good distance from one another. Now imagine that each of us is in our own boat. My life is my boat, and your life is your boat. If the water is unstirred, our lives remain unchanged and unaffected by other boats. You and I remain on the course God has laid out for us, charted before time began. Ideally, our life is without any blemish, misdirection, or change of course.

However, like I said, we are *all* in the ocean of life. The Good. The Bad. The Ugly. When one person acts outside of their God-course, it makes waves. Honestly, we are all broken people in broken relationships in a broken world. This produces a lot of ripples on a daily basis that we have to consider each time we redirect our course. When you begin to recognize how one person's actions affect the entire ocean of boats, you see how we are all connected. The waves carry onto boats close by, then the waves continue and ripples even reach out to boats far off in the distance, reaching people that never even saw the boat where the waves began. Now, all boats affected by these waves are off course. Their God-course is now changed by no permission or effort of their own. And it happens that quickly; one person's choice immediately and long-term, directly and indirectly, rocks other boats, changing their courses and impacting their lives.

Do not fear! I want to give you good news. You are still in your boat. You haven't fallen out and are still at the helm (wheel) of your boat. You can navigate in these rough waters. We can't change the waters, but we can get a grip on the wheel, aim in the direction we want to go, and control our boat to right our course.

There have been days I felt powerless in my boat. Crawling on the floor and letting the waves toss me where they want me to go. But we can't do that forever. We have to stand up, grab the wheel, and aim in a new direction from where the rough waters have taken us. This is a chance for you to go to your mind's eye. Imagine the waters you are in. Are they rough or smooth? Are there other boats around you? Are you at the wheel of your own vessel? Are you at peace or scared? Where is your vessel aiming? Can you see your new God-course?

The ripple effect is a strong visual of how we are all connected. Others impact your life, your life impacts your children's lives, and their lives impact their friends' lives, and so on. When we begin to see how experience, relationships, and lives are interconnected and how we can positively impact them, we gain insight. I hope you are feeling better in knowing you are already on the journey of healing and insight. With the foundation that life is about the journey and knowing the value in insight, you are gaining freedoms you didn't before have.

These freedoms can help parents become healthy people so that they can parent each child according to the child's needs, not the parents' unresolved issues. This book will not cover it all but will get you started. It will spark in you the desire to know yourself more. The desire to know your children more. My desire is that you will use the questions you find and topics you read about to pause, ask yourself the questions, listen for an answer, and respond gently. The wonderful thing is that you have already begun the journey. And now you are on the journey with insight as your tool.

Questions to Ponder

1. In what areas of your *personal life* do you feel you need to develop new insights?

2. In what areas of your *parenting life* do you feel you need to develop insights?

3. What did you learn from reading the definitions of terms to be used in the remainder of this book? How were they different from your previous understanding of these terms?

4. How did the analogy of the ripple effect help you understand how your past unresolved issues might affect your parenting in the present?

Activities

1. What insight or insights did you gain from this chapter? Take some time to write this in your journal.

2. In your journal, write down where you might have difficulty trusting the process as you proceed through this book?

Chapter 3

Calm, Cool, and Collected

What comes to mind when I say calm? How about cool? What about collected? *Calm, cool, and collected* is not merely a cliché. These are three traits that can help you on the journey of life. They provide you with the ability to respond to situations rather than react. As parents it is essential for us to have the ability to stay calm in the midst of chaos. Believe me, this is not a guarantee and is not possible 100 percent of the time. We must first have the skill to do something before we can expect to be able to do it. So, without the skills to be the calm in a storm, we can never expect to be calm.

Staying cool is not letting heat, fire, or anger overcome you. Calm is maintaining inner peace and keeping your nerves and blood pressure under control. Being collected is the ability to keep composure of your behavior even if inside you are not calm or cool. With practice, anyone can at any time practice at least one of these.

Consider firefighters. Like military personnel they are trained to stay calm in the midst of danger. They literally run into a fire. But before they ever get into a fire, they train in a classroom, where there is no fire, to learn what to do when in the midst of a fire. Once trained, they practice their skills in controlled settings. Finally, they courageously venture into fires to save lives and minimize damage. This is a phenomenal tool—to stay calm in the midst of danger. Calm is an internal state of peace resulting in the ability to process and tolerate situations or stressors around you. The word *calm* is a state of being that begins in the mind. Just like firefighters, we as parents can train to remain calm, cool, and collected in the midst of crisis or danger.

As a therapist, I love to help clients experience a state of calm during sessions. While in session, we may use relaxation, visualization, and hypnotherapy to find peace. I believe peace can be found for everyone. Peace is rooted in one's faith in a higher power and transcends circumstance. You have the ability to find peace and carry it with you daily. Accessing and maintaining peace is essential to healthy and insightful parenting. A peaceful state of mind can minimize the impact of stress that happens in life and the power your past has over your life.

Speaking of the past, the first two chapters may have stirred some things from your past that you are not quite sure how to handle or process. This chapter will explain several coping strategies, techniques to calm the body and mind, that can be used daily as a healthy self-care plan or in the midst of crisis when you feel negative emotions. Use these coping skills to help with any stress you may be experiencing. If you are currently feeling well and not under a large amount of stress, begin to practice these skills apart from crisis so they will come more easily when you do experience crisis. Begin to focus on the goal of being and experiencing calm, even remaining calm in the midst of crisis. Once you are able to maintain a level of calm within yourself, then your goal becomes sharing your calm with others who are experiencing negative emotions. Emotions are contagious and so is peace.

Self-Care

As parents we have a tendency to neglect ourselves for the needs of our family. It is important to take care of ourselves so we can care for our family. Self-care is the intentional effort to take care of oneself mentally, physically, and spiritually. Do you have a self-care plan? A self-care plan helps you maintain emotional wellness. A healthy you is the best you to give your children. Self-care includes activities that improve your mind, body, or spirit health. Consider the things you like to do. If they are healthy, do you do them often enough to benefit your well-being?

Simply maintaining good personal hygiene is part of a self-care plan. Showers and baths are stress reducing for many individuals. A healthy sleep pattern is crucial. Research says an average of about eight hours is best for adults. While this can be especially hard for new parents, and sometimes parents of children and teens, it is important to focus on what you can do and what you have control over and manage these. When my children were young, I mastered the power nap during some days and considered three solid hours at night a good night's sleep. Also, nutritional foods and physical exercise can improve overall health. Maintaining contact with loved ones is also proven to improve overall health. Counseling is also used to maintain positive emotional health. Begin to think about your personal needs and develop a self-care plan that creates a healthy, whole you for you and your family.

The above physical needs are essential and basic. Next, I will guide you through techniques to help improve your mental and spiritual well-being. Too often we take care of the physical but neglect our mental and spiritual health. So many people eat well and exercise, but remain riddled with anxiety. While eating and exercise are elements of self-care, the intention behind what we do plays a huge part in how our efforts benefit us as a whole. If self-care techniques are a dreaded task for you, then you will not receive the benefits and will continue to feel anxious or depressed. Even if initially your self-care feels like a task, if your intention is to develop a healthy routine to benefit your whole self, you are on the right track. Your perspective on self-care will determine your results. Self-care is a gift you give yourself because you and your family deserve the best you God has made.

Grounding Techniques

A grounding technique helps to anchor a person in the present. It grounds an individual to the "now." Look around the room. What do you see? Where are you and what are you wearing? Think about what you are sitting on. What material is it made from? What color is it? These types of questions bring you into the present and help you get out of your mind and into reality. If a soldier is in front of me, telling me his story from combat, I will consistently help him remember he is in the room with me and presently is safe and not in danger. Recognizing the walls, chair, color of the room, and texture of the couch helps the brain reset and come back to the room. Grounding is best used when experiencing anxious feelings or nervous thoughts. Look around and identify where you are and at least five details around you. Then name five more details. You are now grounded in the present.

Grounding techniques are useful when you may be triggered by a situation that reminds you of a past memory and you begin to experience anxiety. As you observe and recognize details around you, and remind yourself you are in the present, you then "own" your life and remind your mind that the past is in the past.

Deep Breathing

Deep breathing is great to reduce depression and anxiety. It is the body's built-in stress reliever. Different from involuntary chest breathing, deep breathing, also known as abdominal or belly breathing, is intentional and mindful. My technique of deep breathing is an eight-count model. Read the following steps and then put down the book and try it.

With your mouth closed, breathe in through your nose for the count of three. One, two, three. Then open your mouth and release through your mouth for the count of five. One. Two. Three. Four. Five. When you inhale, fill up your chest cavity completely. It should rise and expand. Then exhale for a count of five. You will feel your chest deflate and your stomach relax as you expel the last amounts of air in your lungs. Keep your inhale shorter than the exhale. When we inhale we are tense; when we exhale we are relaxing. This is why people hold their breath when they are afraid. The fight-or-flight mode of the brain won't exhale because it has to relax to do so. Practice this breathing exercise now. Inhale: 1, 2, 3. Exhale: 1, 2, 3, 4, 5.

The benefits to deep breathing are both voluntary and involuntary. When you decide to deep breathe, you once again own control over your body and your circumstances. In the midst of a panic attack, deep breathe. In the midst of intense grieving, deep breathe. Your choice to breathe and control your breath gains power over your emotions, rather than your emotions gaining power over you. Additionally, deep breathing increases oxygen to your blood and organs and slows your mind, allowing you to process with reason and logic rather than with raw emotion.

Nature

Nature has a way of resetting things. It has natural healing properties. It is both rhythmic and routine. While things might seem spontaneous at time, the longer you sit and watch nature, you realize it is all a routine. Birds fly, trees grow, the sun shines, and wind blows. A trip to the beach engages your senses as you feel the sea breeze across your face, warmth of the sun, and sounds of the waves as they rush in and roll out. A trip to the mountains reveals the serenity of how peaks and valleys coexist, while morning fog and cool winter air engage the senses. These experiences often temporarily interrupt our day, causing us to stop and reflect. (Ever been stopped by the beauty of a sunset or a rainbow while sitting in late-afternoon traffic?) Nature is where we go to get away from the speed and motion of our everyday lives. Embracing even a moment in our natural world offers coping benefits because it relaxes us and draws our focus outward, yet resets us inwardly at the same time. Nature reminds us that our world is full of life and we are a part of it.

The rhythm of nature's routine reminds us we are not as big as we think we are. The world is happening around us, and life always continues. Whether you watch from your window or travel to the sea, spending time in nature is another coping strategy that can be used daily or to combat negative feeling and thoughts. Simple things like walking to get the mail, opening your window, and having live plants or animals in your home can all help you stay connected with nature.

Exercise

Exercise is simply movement of the body. Walking and running are basic forms of exercise. Yoga and Pilates, cross-training and using weights, biking and kickboxing—these are all different forms of physical movement with varying intensity. The latest craze is high-intensity, military-style exercise classes. Whatever exercise you choose, scientific evidence supports its role and benefits in total body wellness. Research shows that daily exercise can reduce stress and depression. An appropriate amount of regular exercise can produce the same results as antidepressants. (However, if you are on medication, do not get off of it without a doctor's permission, and be sure to consult your doctor before starting exercise.) Whatever you are able to do, include exercise in your self-care plan. Exercise is great for regular self-care and also combats an increase in anxious or negative thoughts. In college, if I had a long stent of studying, I would take breaks to exercise. I knew I needed to be calm to process what I was learning.

Avoid excuses to not exercise by making the first steps practical and realistic. Exercise doesn't have to be 5:00 a.m. trips to the gym. If you have animals, walk them daily. If you go shopping, park at the far end of the parking lot. Take the stairs instead of the elevator. I remember reading an article telling busy moms to do twenty-five squats every time they were in the bathroom. Next time you watch a show, instead of speeding through the commercials, try planks, push-ups, or sit-ups instead.

Distraction

When I work with youth, impulsivity is an issue. And when we are impulsive, we tend to get fixed on a certain person or idea. Distraction is a technique used for little children when they can't have what they want. When we know they can't have what they are fixated on, we give them something else to focus on, and this distraction generally works. At our core we all just want to be pleased. Like children wanting a toy, when we experience a problem we tend to replay it over and over again. Rehearsing the negative fuels our negative thoughts and feelings. My recommendation is to distract your brain with something that will flood your mind to forget what you were fixated on. Think of a few things you can flood your mind with, like music, exercise, reading, praying, or crafting. The other techniques in the chapter can also be good positive distractions. Find something you can control in order to turn away from the negative thinking, and enjoy the boost to your mood.

This type of distraction is not the type that leads to procrastination. Its clinical term is "redirection." It is not a negative concept but a short-term coping tool to keep you from acting impulsively in the moment. However, distraction is not a long-term solution; counseling is. Distraction is for immediate refocusing to help you cope in the midst of a stressful situation to get you through until your mood improves and you can address the issue in better ways. It is important to not react in the midst of emotion. Remember, coping skills get us through raw emotion so we can respond with reason and logic. Distraction is a tool to help us diffuse our emotional surge to be able to respond to a situation.

Music

Music has power. It creates mood. Classical music is shown to increase focus and is great for studying. Pop culture music has been shown to increase energy. Spiritual music feeds the soul. Whatever type of music you choose, music influences your mood. Choose wisely. If you are inclined to depression, fill your mind with positive music and messages. Every sound has a message. Listening to positive music daily helps manage stress. Also, in the midst of greater times of stress, listening to music is a method to shift your mind and focus on something that energizes and positively impacts you.

Relaxation

Relaxation is so essential and seldom practiced. Relaxation is simply the state of relaxing. To relax is to allow yourself to rest. Resting is especially hard for parents. Many parents feel guilty if they allow themselves time to rest. Never feel guilty about self-care. Relaxation allows the body to reset. Giving our bodies permission to relax allows us to maintain the natural rhythm of movement and rest. When relaxed, we can remain calm regardless of our circumstance. We can relax at the beach or in the mountains. We can relax at our house or in the car. Sometimes pulling into a parking space for five minutes before you pick up your child from school—to close your eyes, relax, and breathe—can pull you into the positive. If you only have free time in the bathroom or when you walk and get your mail, or if a situation suddenly builds around you, use the deep-breathing technique to relax and calm your mind. Even small moments of relaxation in your day can give you the peace you need to finish your day strong.

Mindfulness

Mindfulness is a deeper level of relaxation and draws our attention to a singular object or thought. While you are in a relaxed state, begin to focus your attention on your breathing. Do not try to change your breathing; just allow it to flow in and out of your body while you observe it. You do not have to try to breathe; your body knows what it needs to do. Simply pay attention to the rhythm of each breath. Mindfulness is a technique that not only encourages relaxation but also trains the mind that you have control over it. When we feel out of control, we let our thoughts control us. Mindfulness reverses this concept as we choose what to focus on.

Progressive Muscle Relaxation (PMR)

This technique is great to tackle stress that your body physically stores in your muscles. PMR is the process of tightening and releasing the muscles in your body. Like deep breathing, we cannot be tense when exhaling. Muscles cannot hold stress when they are relaxed. PMR focuses on the body and forces the body to relax areas where it is tense. Your mind is focused on commanding the body what to do. Read through the following steps and then try this on your own.

To begin PMR, first tighten up all the muscles in your body. Now release them. This is the two-step process. Tighten and release. Next, with the following muscle groups one at a time, do the same two-step process three times for each muscle group. Neck and shoulders. Arms and hands. Back and abdomen. Thighs and butt. Calves and feet. Finally, toes. Repeat the two-step process on any body part that still feels tense. This can be done anytime anywhere, but the calmer your environment, the more benefit you will derive from PMR.

Safe Place

A safe place is a visual place in your mind where you go when you want to feel safe. This is a place where you know you can relax. My safe place is at the beach. I love the beach for its multisensory experience of peace. I remember the beach and choose to visualize this as my safe place. Your safe place can be a place you have been before where you felt an ultimate sense of peace. Or it may be a place you can imagine and have never been. It is a place where you feel security and perhaps the warmth of genuine love. It may be a childhood memory that brings an overwhelming sense of warmth, acceptance, and peace. There are no rules to your safe place except it is only for you. There is no danger in your safe place. When you picture your safe place in your mind, take a few deep breaths while you keep your mind focused on your safe place. Safe places are best when we need something good to focus on. It can be used during relaxation, deep breathing, or distraction. It can be used in a moment of experiencing stress or as a daily practice to improve overall mood.

Practice this now. Visualize your safe place and recognize the benefit and calm of being in your safe place. What are you feeling and how calm is your mind? Recognize these feelings, accept these feelings as part of you, and take them with you as you go about your day. Your safe place is evidence to you that you know what safe feels like.

Journaling

There is power in the written word. When we put pencil to paper and write out our thoughts and feelings, we gain freedom. Writing for self-care is usually done in journal style and can focus on a variety of topics. Give yourself permission to put to paper what you are feeling. If you are mad, write about it. If you are happy, write about it. When something goes right or wrong, journal the success and failures of life so you can own it as part of your life story. Keep your journal between you and God, and let it be a safe place for you to be honest with yourself. As you work through this book, use a journal to process and digest what you read.

Journaling will also help you build your parenting tools. You can see your progress and successes. Your journals provide a place to look back and be reminded of the insights you learned about yourself and your children. We all need a place to process and freely reflect on what may be happening in our lives and our children's lives. Journaling can be short and succinct, or lengthy and memoir-like.

Prayer

Prayer changes things and it brings peace. Simply put, prayer is talking to God. Sending your grumbles and gratitude to God in an effort to maintain spiritual health. Prayer is a conscious act of acknowledging our own limitations in this life and includes a God who is the same yesterday, today, and forever. The submission of prayer brings comfort and peace because we understand we are only human, and some things need superhuman strength and intervention.

There is an old saying: "You don't find atheists in foxholes." This alludes to the idea that everyone seeks God in times of trouble. But truly, prayer can be a part of your daily life, to remind and accept that you may be on a journey, but God sees the entire map. While many pray for answers, it is often the act of prayer that changes things. You may include your family or loved ones in prayer—not only to pray for them but also to ask them to pray for you and your needs. This builds up our interpersonal relationships, which is another source of coping.

Support System

A support system is a group of individuals who support you mentally, emotionally, and physically—people who you rely on for advice and encouragement. You may already know who these people are, or you may need to develop a support system. It is good to let your support people know who they are and that you value their relationship in your life. Some may see it as an honor; others see it as a burden. Due to the emotional and mental needs we may have at times, we should allow our friends and loved ones to let us know any limitations in providing support. You might list these people in the front of your journal, so that when you have an awesome day and want to share it with someone, or when you can't get out of a negative mindset and need to talk, you can call someone in your support system. It is important to have the right people in your support system. We will discuss more about relationships in the next chapter.

Safety Plan

Some parents reading this book are still in survival mode, so any talk about journaling and PMR seems frivolous if you are just focused on literally being safe. For you, it is necessary to develop a safety plan, a course of action to keep you and your children safe if necessary. Whether the danger is natural disaster, hunger, abuse, or worse, you deserve to be safe. Whether a friend or family, call one person and make a plan with them about how to prevent the danger from happening in your life and your children's lives. It may mean you need to seek shelter or professional counseling. Professional counselors and local abuse hotlines are well-equipped to help you ensure your own and your children's safety.

Am Safe vs. Feel Safe

I want to leave you with an activity that I believe helps with the calm, cool, and collected mindset. Being safe and feeling safe are two different things. "Am safe" is about the actual fact of being safe. Being safe is about people, places, and things that pose no imminent risk to us. The risk can be a physical, mental, or emotional threat. But if there is no imminent threat, you are safe.

"Feel safe" is about the feeling of being safe. This is not rooted in fact but feeling. Depending on past experience our "feel safe" may tend to be positive or negative toward life and can confuse us. We may feel safe in a rocking chair if we have good memories of them. Conversely, we may not feel safe in a car if we have been in an accident before. How our mind associates a current experience with the same experience in our past is how "feel safe" can get confused. Although we are safe in the car, we do not feel safe because we are still connecting being in the car now (present) with being in an accident (past).

"Feel safe" is only a problem when it does not line up with the "am safe" reality. In short, if we do not feel safe, we tend to think we are not safe. If these beliefs are distorted and are affecting our lives, we have to discern and correct the false beliefs between "am safe vs. feel safe."

Acknowledging the things that you do and do not feel safe about is key in keeping calm. Next time you feel anxious, look around and ask yourself: Where is the danger? Is it real? Am I safe? If you are actually safe, take a breath and practice one of the techniques discussed in the chapter. Beginning to process your internal fears will help you cope with your own needs and your children's needs.

Moving Forward

Life is stressful, but we don't have to be stressed about life. Coping skills and managing stress are essential to life. The techniques in this chapter are just a snapshot of the abundance of coping skills available. I believe those listed here are the simplest to practice on a daily basis and in the midst of crisis. Review the chapter and decide what techniques fit best for you. What techniques do you plan to use on a daily basis? What techniques will help you best in the midst of crisis? Just like the firefighter, when these skills become routine in your life, they will become instinct and be a natural coping behavior when you are in the midst of crisis.

In these first three chapters, you have begun to accept the journey as well as develop more insight. For much of our children's lives, we are the driver and they are the passengers. The healthy insights we develop as parents provides an example for our children and lays a strong foundation for them as they begin to journey on their own as adults. Finally, adding coping skills to your parent toolbox will better equip you for what lies ahead.

Questions to Ponder

1. Do you currently have a self-care plan? If so, how has it helped you in the past? If not, what has kept you from creating one and following it?

2. Which of the listed self-care techniques do you want to incorporate into your daily life?

3. How can you begin to use these techniques to keep yourself calm, cool, and collected?

Activities:

1. Complete the "Am Safe vs. Feel Safe" exercise in appendix B.

2. Write down your self-care plan and goals for beginning to implement them in your life.

3. Write down the names of those in your support system in the front of your journal, and contact them to make sure they know you will call on them in times of stress or crisis.

PART 2

ESSENTIALS

With a foundation of knowledge, and the tools to begin this journey to wholeness, we must move forward in three areas of life that create the greatest challenges as parents—relationships, family, and feelings. All of these are central to our lives, and when we understand how they affect us and our choices, we are able to overcome the challenges and obstacles that face us as individuals and parents.

Because we were created for community, we live our lives in relationship. Family, friends, coworkers, even acquaintances—all affect how we see ourselves, and in turn, how we care for our children. We'll explore the ways we can create the healthiest relationships possible.

Family is the heart of our relationships, which may make it even harder to be healthy and balanced as we parent. We'll take the time to break down the way we "do" family and find the places where new insights can lower stress and increase joy.

Feelings are essential parts of who we are as people, but they can also bring a world of pain and hurt if not understood and expressed in a healthy manner. The journey to becoming a more insightful parent runs through our emotional selves, and leads to a place of hope.

Chapter 4

Relationships

Remember, we are all boats in the same ocean. Our actions cause a ripple effect to other boats around us. Some boats are closer to yours than others, and you are closer to some boats than others. That proximity, that closeness in our relationships, means that the waves of our actions and reactions have a greater ripple effect on the boats close to us. It is healthy to acknowledge the distance you have between some boats and the closeness you have toward others.

Relationships are key to a healthy view of our children and ourselves. Earlier we learned that relationships help us develop at different stages and meet different needs. Erikson defined the virtues gained through the stages of development as hope, will, purpose, competency, fidelity, love, care, and wisdom. These stages require connection, and connection only happens in relationship, especially in our close family relationships. Maslow established the criteria for basic, psychological, and self-fulfillment needs—all of which require relationship to achieve.

Boundaries

When we begin to understand that needs are met through relationships, it is also important to learn what healthy relationships look like. All sporting events have rules to the game. The rules keep it fair for all players and allow the game to be well understood by spectators and players alike. Just like sports, relationships have rules. These are called *boundaries* and it is a key tool for healthy family and relationships. Boundaries are guidelines, parameters, and limits for someone or something. A bedtime for a young child is a boundary. Limiting phone time for a teenager during the week is a boundary. Limiting work calls while you are with family is a boundary. These are all practical boundaries that research shows make for a well-balanced life. However, boundaries become harder to establish when they are about intangible things we cannot see or touch. For example, you can choose to not engage in an argument when someone is yelling at you. Or show respect to others by not yelling in a heated discussion. Or choose to end a long-winded negative conversation because you are becoming emotionally unhealthy. Or you can help your child learn how to choose friends who make good decisions. These are boundaries that have lasting and profound effects on our lives and leave a legacy of positive examples for our children.

Many of these intangible boundaries are relational boundaries, which are boundaries within relationships. Boundaries can be restrictive or nonexistent. They can be love-based or fear-based. Boundaries can be self-defeating or self-accepting, intentional or unintentional. We approach others and they approach us based on the boundaries we display. We must acknowledge that our own life experiences can create the boundaries we live by. We often live by relationship boundaries we don't even know we have. As we develop insight we begin to see these boundaries and how they may be healing or hindering relationships in our lives.

For example, Susan came into my office with concern for her sister. She wanted a close relationship with her sister, but felt the phone calls and efforts were only one way. She said every time she called, the conversation was great and everything seemed fine. But Susan shared that once she had a child, and since her sister was protective of her own children, for the first couple years, the sister didn't allow Susan to bring her child for a visit with its cousins. As a result, even now, when Susan's sister does call, it is usually to ask if Susan can watch her children. But Susan feels that even though her niece and nephew are older, her own child is not welcomed. She assumes this boundary even though her sister has not stated it. This is an example of how past experience can create boundaries in our lives that may not even exist.

Roles

Relationships are seldom as clear as sporting events. The rules in sporting events help players know what they can and cannot do. Boundaries help individuals know what is and is not appropriate in relationships. Assigning players positions in games help others know what is expected of that individual in the game. Coaches assign players to positions based on their natural ability or skill. In relationships, we also give assignments to individuals; this is called roles. Roles, like boundaries, can be constricting and devaluing if misused or abused. Just as a captain can throw his power around and ruin team morale, abusing a role in a relationship also steals the beauty of equality and security for individuals in the relationship. It can be difficult when we assign roles to people in our lives rather than allowing individuals to naturally fill a role.

A role is different than a title. We are all a husband, wife, mother, daughter, son, parent, etc. But if you were only one of those things, what would that look like? A husband to me could look very different than a husband to you. I may say a husband should mow the lawn, be the primary breadwinner, and take me on dates. You may think otherwise. While none of these things are bad, the key word here is *should*. When we use the word *should*, we assign a person's value to a task. To maintain and develop healthy relationships, avoid use of the word *should*.

Expectations

Roles are often created by expectations and experiences, based on what the relationships around us looked like in the past. Expectations are often created by the unstated "shoulds" we place on individuals that we assign certain roles to. By assigning a role to someone, we elevate our expectations over the relationship. Not every relationship needs roles for the individuals in the relationship.

What I expect from someone I am in relationship with is called *relational expectations*. Relational expectations are seldom discussed, and too many relationships are destroyed by unmet expectations. We have to evaluate the expectations we have for ourselves and for our family and friends. Ask yourself if your expectations are realistic or idealistic and whether these relational expectations are helpful or harmful in our lives. Too often we get caught in a cycle of unrealistic expectations and we feel like a failure to others and ourselves. We feel others have failed us because we have too many "shoulds" in our vocabulary. Once we recognize and dismiss the shoulds from relationships, we can than evaluate the health of the relationship. Simply put, you shouldn't should on yourself. And you shouldn't should on others either.

"Shoulding" happens so much with new moms. "I should be happy. I should love my baby. He/she should be sleeping through the night. He/she should be eating. I should be nursing." To this I say: Stop it. New moms often have this exhaustive and impossible list of expectations built from all the shoulds of others, society, media, and their own beliefs. As we've said before, parenthood is hard enough, and with obstacles like shoulds in the way, we will see even simple struggles as failures.

Expectations in relationships are created from our good and bad experiences in life. As you identify in yourself the expectations you have for yourself and others, you might notice an odd sense of nervousness or sadness associated with some expectations, and you can't figure out why. Sometimes our inner mind (unconscious) develops beliefs about people and relationships that we are not aware of on the surface. Such expectations may arise from crisis or secondary trauma, and they can cause us to react and relate differently to those close to us.

It's Your Birthday

Boundaries are built from expectations, and expectations define roles of individuals. These things all indicate who we're comfortable sharing information with, and remind us that we share different things with different people. We can accept that this is okay and actually quite a healthy way to have relationships in our lives.

A visualization to help distinguish the relationships in our lives is a three-tier birthday cake. You are represented by the topper, and the people in your life are represented by the three tiers of cake. Imagine it's your birthday. Not just any birthday but the best possible birthday. I want you to imagine your loved ones are there. The ones you know truly care about you. They can be friends, family, or mentors. Perhaps in person or in spirit, the right people are here to celebrate you today—your birthday. The first few people to arrive are the ones you rely most on. They build you up and speak honesty into your life, which helps you become a healthier person. These people belong on your top tier, the tier closest to you. You know who belongs here. You know who loves, supports, and encourages you. When they speak truth, it is to help you become a better person. They build you up, not tear you down.

Now, I want you to imagine the guest list just got a little longer. Perhaps some people come to your party whose company you enjoy from time to time, but they are not your "go-to" when you need support and encouragement. Still, they are in good moods and the conversation is light, so the party is still hoppin'. These individuals belong on your cake's middle tier. They are next in line for support, and there are more of them because you generally share less with them. These relationships are not as deep as those on your top tier.

Third, imagine the people who are part of your life but more distant, with few and not always positive interactions. But the party is grand, so you decided they should be invited too. Move these onto the bottom cake tier in your visual. They may play a slightly more negative or neutral, rather than supportive, role in your life. These relationships are shallow, and you share few intimate details with them.

Visualizing your birthday cake helps you recognize and accept that you are in control of the roles and relationships people have in your life. Take a moment now and to write out this exercise on a piece of paper or perhaps in your journal (see appendix C). There is power in the action of putting pen to paper. Draw the three-tier cake and assign people to each layer accordingly. In general, do not include everyone in your life, only the people you have regular contact with or who have played a significant role in your life's story. Look at your cake and evaluate it. These layers are intentional, conscious boundaries you have in your life. You can see the difference between the people on the top and middle tiers and how close they are to you. You know the different types of information you are comfortable sharing with a person according to the tier they are on. It is your right and privilege to determine who is safe and where they belong in your life. Remember, these decisions and steps are always working toward a healthy you. If this activity has stirred up some hurt and painful feelings, write about it, go back to the coping strategies in chapter 3, and work through it.

As you reflect on your personal boundaries for individuals in your life, how do you feel? What are you thinking? I know for me, I was initially conflicted with guilt and relief. I felt guilty that I was putting people in order and deciding where they belong. And I felt relief because I was deciding a person's level of closeness and influence in my life. Evaluating relationships can be a healthy practice and help determine our own contributions in the lives of others as well. When you do this exercise, if you feel guilty, process it. Remember, you do have the right to determine a healthy role for all individuals in your life. The key word is *healthy*. An arrogant teen, whose rebellion has them putting their parents lowest on the cake, is not processing from a healthy position and therefore the decision is not good for them or their parent. Our boundaries and relationships are dramatically impacted by our views and perspectives at the time. The same experience can mean different things to the same person at different points in their lives depending on our perspective or feelings at the time.

Keep the Whole Picture in Mind

Our lives can also be visualized as an intricate puzzle. The key to living from a healthy place in relationships is to keep the whole puzzle in mind. This means we think about the big picture, while also valuing all the little experiences. This is how we examine our relationships and boundaries. Some pieces seem to be made for another puzzle. Other pieces are corner pieces and keep the puzzle grounded, while some pieces hold the intimate details of the picture. But all pieces have a place in the big picture. That is a picture of healthy relationships—parts with details and parts with boundaries, but where all fit together to make a picture of the relationship. Understanding the puzzle pieces and knowing where they fit comes when we can process them based on facts and not feelings.

One may say, "My mother has always been supportive to me in my life, so she belongs on the top tier of my cake." This is likely supported by the mother investing time, love, and attention into her child. Another experience may be that a child's grandmother verbally harassed her in front of the neighborhood kids so the child (or adult) determines that the grandmother belongs on her third tier. This too is valid.

Our cake is for our own well-being. I may place my sister on my top tier, but she places me on the middle tier. What matters to me is where I feel safe in placing someone on my cake. Where someone places me on their cake is of little consequence if I am practicing healthy boundaries. Our placement on each other's cakes is not significant. However, it can become significant if we feel someone does not have healthy boundaries and we feel pulled too close or pushed away. In that case, process how you feel about it and if it changes your comfort level and where you believe that person belongs on your cake.

Awareness and application of roles, boundaries, and expectations in relationships can dramatically change your journey. Your life may be redirecting itself as you begin to process and make healthy decisions through these exercises. You may be on a strong, healthy course and these activities will equip you to continue the journey. The purpose and benefit is to improve your emotional and mental well-being. When something good happens in your life, this means things are changing. Therefore, many of our relationships will experience change as well.

Relationships constantly evolve and change. They grow or fade depending on the choices made by individuals in the relationship. Remember, relationships take two individuals. As you establish new boundaries and awareness, the change may not be well received. When healthy choices are not well received, you need to take time away from that relationship. This is often seen in unhealthy relationships when one individual decides they want to change things, and the other is not ready for change. Even good change can produce fear in people. Remember that change takes time. I'm proud of you making it this far into the book. From learning about the journey and the value of insight to coping skills and evaluating relationships, these are huge issues you have examined and you now have great tools to continue on in the process.

Questions to Ponder

1. In the discussion of relationships, what issues arose for you that you might need to deal with regarding past or present relationships in your life?

2. What roles and expectations have others placed on you that you need to address in order to create healthy boundaries?

3. What roles and expectations have you placed on others that have been an unnecessary burden or were wrongly

imposed? How did or does that affect those relationships?

4. What boundaries for yourself, your children, or others need to change to create healthier environments and relationships?

Activities:

1. Write down in your journal an insight or insights you received in this chapter and how it will change the way you live or parent.

2. If you have not yet completed the exercise of the birthday cake in appendix C, fill out your birthday cake tiers, listing those who are in those various relationship levels in your life. Evaluate which ones might need to move up or down in your tiers and why.

Chapter 5

Family

Family and relationships are in many ways interchangeable. It is hard to talk about family without talking about relationships in general. Our families affect our relationships and our relationships affect our families. In fact, our first relational experiences are with family. We learn how to speak and how to listen. We learn facial expressions and body language. Some skills are taught and some merely observed. Looking back, you may see the relational skills you choose to keep and those you chose to purge. These original foundational experiences and relationships in our lives developed who we are. This chapter will focus on helping you gain insight to how your family of origin has shaped you and help you decide how you will shape your own family unit.

If you look up the definition of the word *family*, there are literally twenty interpretations of the word. For this text, *family* is a group of individuals, biologically related or not, that you are connected to or related to in some way. A family can live under one roof. A family can be across the world from one another. My children have "aunts" and "uncles" who are not related by blood but by love. Your *family of origin* is the family you were raised in, the family you spent most of your childhood with. This can be one or several family units, depending on your experience. Your *family unit* is your current family, the group of individuals to which you are connected now.

People generally react in one of two ways to the word *family*: good or bad. This is not a right or wrong answer, simply a reaction based on perspectives and experiences. A neutral association to family likely means there were unmet needs to some extent and the individual has detached themselves. Remember, reactions are less developed than responses, and learning how to control them will help us on the journey of insight. Just like relationships, we can use the birthday cake and ripple effect metaphors to assess how our family has influenced us and what boundaries we desire to have with them.

Remember that our experiences create our boundaries and our boundaries dictate what our relationships look like. The value we place on family is directly related to how we have experienced family both as a child and as an adult. Our awareness of what is a healthy family can start at what we learned in chapter 1 about virtues and needs. We know that hope is developed after a child learns trust. A child learns trust by having basic needs provided for. If these essentials are met, the child feels safe and will view family as safe. Our view of family can change as our experiences change. It is important to not only recognize the family we are currently in but also to reflect and identify the experiences we had growing up to begin to process how our family of origin still influences our current family unit. As an adult, you now have the power and choice to reflect on your life as a child and decide the life you want for your own children. Some experiences may not be preventable, but how you respond to life's curve balls, and even line drives at times, will help your children learn the coping skills they need when they parent their own children. This process of self-reflection and application is insightful parenting.

Family memories are important because they shape our expectations of our own family unit. If we have good family memories from our childhood, we want to replicate them for our children. If we have negative memories, we want to avoid repeating them. Recognizing the good and bad of the past and deciding to replicate the good and avoid the bad requires insight. Begin to reflect on your own childhood and the things you enjoyed. What things would you replicate for your children? What lessons did you learn that will help your children?

As a child, I was happy. I played sports, excelled in school, and had friends. My parents were married during my childhood years, and I remember eating dinner around the family table. One time we as a family of seven were at the dinner table eating spaghetti. I remember the blue drapes behind the traditional wood rectangle table. Well, in a fit of humor, mimicking a scene from *Mr. Mom*, I flung spaghetti sauce across the table onto the drapes. In a kind gesture, my mother corrected me but didn't act harshly in any way. How my mother responded to my behavior helped me learn to give grace to my children in moments of childlike impulsivity.

The previous experience with my mother and sitting with my family around the dinner table are memories I want to pass on to my children. If I replicated most of my childhood for my children to experience, they might turn out okay, maybe even better than "okay," because I was able to laugh, grow, live, and most of all, experience life. I am able to recognize the good and how it has shaped me. This is insight.

As we know, however, life is never perfect. Struggles and negative memories challenge our definition of *family*. When I began to reflect on my life, I didn't want my children to experience the painful parts of my childhood. The rejection I felt. The shame I carried. I didn't want my children to experience life as unsafe. Unfortunately, these experiences created a negative perceived reality, which I carried into parenthood. Thankfully, with help, I soon took a long look at my own life. I realized I was living "expecting" something bad to happen. This realization caused me to stop, look, and listen before I imposed false expectations on my children.

Negative experiences have a great impact on our view of ourselves; we can have a lifetime of good memories, but just one negative experience, one harsh word, can shatter a healthy view and change our expectations, altering our course once again.

By acknowledging both the good and bad of my childhood, I am able to recognize my own needs and seek healing. I love my children deeply and try to respond, not react, in situations. I talk to them regularly about their right to make healthy boundaries in relationships and for their bodies. I separately take time to listen to them and learn what's going on in their lives. My parenting is not focused on meeting my own needs through my children. If we refuse to take care of our own needs, we can inadvertently push our unmet family needs onto our children. When we acknowledge the root of our expectations, we are able to change the lens through which we view our family.

Looking back, you may have grown up in a healthy, loving, well-balanced home. You may have had brothers and sisters who cherished and cared for you. You may have had a grandmother who nurtured you and taught you how to cook. If this is the case, family may feel good to you. On the other hand, you may have witnessed domestic violence. You may have been placed in foster care. You may have experienced death, loss, or abandonment. You may have been abused. If this is the case, family may not feel good to you. Regardless of your childhood, we are never doomed in our future because of our past. Our view of family can change as we develop insight about how these experiences, good and bad, have affected us.

As you progress through this book, you may be challenged as you recall difficult memories or trigger certain emotional responses. When this happens, remember to revisit the coping skills from chapter 3 to help you navigate your own insights. We cannot feel safe and stressed at the same time. Neither can we absorb information while we are anxious. For the individuals who feel family is not safe, this is the time to establish your coping skills so you can get the most out of this chapter.

Structure and Dynamics

The structure and dynamics we experience in our families shape how we approach the rest of the world. The structure of a family is important to notice and recognize its influence in our lives. Structure is how a family is laid out. What is the design of all individuals in that unit? Who is predominantly in charge? How does the family relate and interact to one another? How are decisions made? What is the work/life balance of the home?

Dynamics are the interactions between individuals: how we listen, talk, communicate, and interact. For instance, a previous generation believed children should be seen and not heard; these children grew to be adults who felt natural guilt for just being themselves. If a child is not to be heard, they learn their voice does not matter and therefore they do not matter. The basic psyche of a child, and the inner mind, is so concrete that messages are converted to life rules, boundaries, and instructions. When these children, who felt they had no value, became parents, the pendulum swung, so they raised their children to speak up and be engaged in adult conversation. This could result in children who ruled the house because Mom didn't want them to be a doormat. The structure and dynamics in these homes do not display a healthy balance of mutual respect and love.

Neither of these positions is ideal. The truth is that healthy is found in the middle. We can only get to the truth through evaluating our own beliefs and actions and exploring their origins.

As we explore the origins of life experiences and look at family dynamics, we have to step back and look at healthy versus normal. Many parents will say to me, "I experienced that and I'm okay. That's just normal." Normal is not always healthy. Healthy is not always normal. This is easy to apply to the food industry. It has become normal in America for a family to eat fast food regularly. Fast food is convenient, fast, and generally tastes good. However, we know that fast food is causing a surge in obesity in America. Obesity is linked to cancer, high blood pressure, cholesterol, and heart attacks. How can something that is normal produce so much harm? Because normal is not synonymous for healthy. Healthy means healthy. Normal means commonplace, but not necessarily healthy. I hope through your own self-discovery and developing healthy family practices, your family normal will also mean healthy.

Responsibility vs. Results

As parents we are endowed with the responsibility and privilege to help little humans grow to be big humans. These small beings in our houses, running through the mud and crashing onto a pile of folded towels, are gifts we get to help grow. While we have our children in our home, we have the responsibility to parent them as best as we are able and hope the best for them. Making a good effort to do all the right things and make the best choices for you and your children will help you know you did the best you could. When you know you have done the best you can, give yourself permission to accept the independence of your child to finish the task. It is your responsibility to teach your child respect and show them love; it is their responsibility to apply respect and love. You cannot own your child's choices unless you intentionally neglect to provide them a healthy example.

Living without regret as a parent is essential in the journey to insightful parenting. Even with all the right choices and honoring the responsibility of parenthood, we cannot control the outcome. We must accept and recognize that while we are responsible for healthy parenting, we cannot guarantee the results for our children. When we get caught in focusing on results, like who our children will become or what they will do as adults, we lose sight of the journey. Healthy parenting balances perspective of the destination on the horizon, while enjoying the ride of parenthood along the way.

A Healthy Model for Family

A healthy family can be created. Our life history does not determine our future. The right framework will guide you toward a healthy model and mindset on family. Beyond basic needs, a healthy family foundation is far less about material things and primarily developed through intangible things. Once basic needs are met, the structure, dynamics, and experiences create the family you and your children deserve. Developing a healthy family is like a recipe. Several ingredients are required, and when you have a good recipe, the whole house is filled with the aroma of whatever is baking in the kitchen. The same is true with a healthy family. When you have the right ingredients, the whole house is filled with the aroma. Love, acceptance, boundaries, support, forgiveness, communication, and faith are some key ingredients for healthy families.

Love

In families, quite often, it is assumed that love is in the home. Assumptions are a terrible thing to live by. Assumptions don't fill a child's heart with love. If love is learned as a child, it is replicated in adulthood and generally natural in one's new family unit. If it is not learned in childhood, it must be learned as an adult and is not a "given" in one's new family unit. Learning to love by giving and receiving as a child and adult look the same. For instance, a child feels loved when listened to or given attention; adults feel loved in the same ways. Love is learned through experiences. Love is a verb. It is an action and builds up the person, never tears down. It is healthy and respects boundaries, is never forceful or violating. Healthy boundaries are a form of love. Positive words are a gesture of endearment. Spending time with someone can fill a heart with joy. Helping to complete a task or chore is a display of love. Physical affection, such as a hug, a kiss, and holding hands, communicates love. Also, gifts and presents can show love to someone. Love is communicated differently for different people.

Acceptance

Being able to accept oneself, flaws and all, is an incredibly liberating experience. Surrounding yourself with individuals who do the same is another sign of a healthy family. Acceptance can come from your family, but sometimes you find it outside of your family. For example, a few years ago, my husband and I were asked to go and be part of a church launch team. While excited, we were going to a new area of town to a congregation that had been together for more than two decades. They were a family. When we arrived, I surveyed the population. I stopped, looked, and listened. I gravitated toward an older woman quite naturally. She and I became supernaturally close in a short time, and I began to call her Mom, and my children called her Nana Isabella. Over the course of two years, my children and I developed a whole new family at this church. They had an aunt and Nana they saw several times a week who loved us, and in turn, we felt accepted. This was the acceptance—pure, full, fun—needed in our life at the time. My husband's family and mine are wonderful, but being in a new place, we needed family there and we found it. A family is a place you can go where you are accepted. We feel accepted when we can be who we truly are and know we are welcomed.

Communication

Good communication skills are essential to a healthy family. Communication is defined as the transmission of an idea from one person to another. This definition is so far from the "communicating" I see happening in families. To transmit an idea is to pass it from one person to another. Like playing catch. If you want to play catch with a friend, you first must both have a glove on and a ball to throw with. The ball is the idea and the glove is how you catch the idea. When a parent disciplines a child, we have to consider: How will my child best learn, or catch, the idea that yelling at their sibling is not appropriate? When we yell, it is likely we are playing a game of dodge ball rather than catch. The problem with dodge ball is that the balls end up smacking someone or on the floor. I don't want to communicate in a manner where all my ideas end up harming others or on the ground.

Healthy communication first seeks to understand how someone will interpret and receive an idea for maximum comprehension before they speak. This is a process of insight into your own and others' communication styles.

Forgiveness

Forgiveness, like family, usually stirs one of two feelings: good or bad. Forgiveness can be a difficult and lengthy process. Yet at other times it can be an immediate decision. Forgiveness, like love, is a verb and a choice. Forgiveness is like an onion. Onions have layers, burn your eyes when you start messing with them, and are really stinky. For many forgiveness is a process with layers, that burns your eyes and is stinky. Forgiveness may be all three things in the process but results in an indescribable sense of self-acceptance and peace. Self-acceptance after forgiveness is essential to move on from negative life events. Unforgiveness still allows our offenders to have power over us.

Forgiveness is accepting the past as it is and no longer trying to change it, because the past will never change. Sometimes forgiveness requires grieving. Often when we need to forgive it is because an offense has happened. So immediately, we may be angry. We can also deny, minimize, bargain, or become depressed, but in the end, the goal for forgiveness is acceptance—acceptance of the event and placing it in the past, giving up the control it has over us.

Children need to see forgiveness in our lives. They also need to see apologies when necessary. If you lose your temper as a parent and yell in the car line, a genuine "I'm sorry. Will you forgive me?" helps your child learn their value, healthy communication, and how to grant forgiveness. What a precious gift that is, to learn to give and receive forgiveness.

Forgiveness is not synonymous with reconciliation. Once you forgive, you then decide whether or not reconciliation is a healthy choice. If there is possible harm of any sort—difficult lifestyles, poor examples, chronic habits, or potential abuse—you can reserve the right to not reconcile. You are developing a healthy you and a healthy family. As you further your insight, determine what level, if any, of reconciliation is appropriate. When reconciliation happens and forgiveness has not been granted, the relationship will likely repeat the cycle of unhealthy behaviors and communication because all parties are not working on their own mental and emotional health.

Faith

Faith is a core principle in healthy families. Faith is belief in something. In marriage, spouses have faith in one another's fidelity. In spirituality, individuals have faith in a power higher than themselves. Whatever your faith is in, be sure it is true. Faith is synonymous with trust. We trust our children, little by little, as years go on. We have faith in the bank to hold our money. But the faith that holds families together needs to be in a source who can answer your deepest, hardest questions. When we are broken people, we can't just depend on our own understanding to get us through. Having a deep faith allows you to explore your feelings, emotions, and experiences, and know there is always something bigger and greater there to catch you and help you through. Faith is another tool to help you navigate life's journey and develop insight.

Seek a Healthy Family

Families and relationships are essential to a healthy life. We know many needs can only be met in relationships. Relationships require boundaries to be healthy, and healthy relationships help us develop insight and improve our lives. *Family* should not be a scary word, but for some it is. With the right ingredients you can redefine family in your life. Make changes to have healthy family relationships; engage the ones you can and limit contact for those who may be harmful. In some cases, it may be necessary to eliminate contact all together. It is empowering to own our role in relationships and essential that we own our part so we can acknowledge the positive roles other people have played in our lives. Developing insight along the journey helps you be the best parent you can be because of, rather than in spite of, life's experiences.

Questions to Ponder

1. What does family mean to you?

2. Which ingredients of the healthy family are you already using? Which ingredients need to be improved or added?

3. If an ingredient for a healthy family is missing for you, what steps can you take to restore it in your family?

Activity

1. In your journal, write down the insight or insights you have discovered in this chapter and how they will change your life or parenting.

2. This week, be intentional about applying two of the healthy ingredients to your family life. Journal what you did and what was the outcome.

Chapter 6
Feelings

I once read a novel about a young woman who inherited a mansion from a distant relative. When she inherited the home, she was unable to move there immediately but would travel there on the weekends. The house overlooked the Pacific Ocean and had beaches and cliffs in its sightline. Every time she visited the home, she discovered something new. She explored the rooms she liked but avoided the ones that gave her discomfort. However, the more she visited, the more comfortable she became, even in the rooms she previously avoided. Eventually she noticed that every room served a different part of her soul. Every room met a need or held a feeling that helped her begin to embrace and accept herself. The mansion helped her accept and integrate the parts of herself and her life that she had closed off. Before she inherited the mansion, she didn't have the insight that she had separated parts of herself to avoid including them in her identity.

As parents we do this a lot with our feelings and memories. We split off parts of ourselves that we do not understand or perhaps do not want to own as part of who we are. When we talk about our feelings, we wish it could be all good, all the time. But just as the woman in the story couldn't control everything she encountered in the mansion, we cannot always anticipate what we may feel in certain situations.

Life is a journey and unpredictable, and feelings are a part of it all. We can't know good without knowing bad. While we experience many wonderful feelings as parents, we do ourselves a disservice if we focus on the good alone. Good experiences and feelings need to be nurtured, but likewise negative feelings need to be processed and understood. If things are going well, and you are insightfully enjoying life, well done. However, far too many of us have past experiences that are barriers to accepting our children and ourselves. Insightful parenting is looking at ourselves as a whole, good and bad, and accepting it all as part of us. The woman in the book finally felt like she was at home when she accepted every room in the house as belonging and fitting into the total package of the house. Some feelings are easier to accept than others.

If it isn't obvious by now, I am an idealist. I love the idea of all things working in unity, without chaos or pain. I love the idea, especially as we think of children, that life doesn't hurt. I love all good and no bad. I believe children should stay in summer all year long and that ice cream doesn't make us fat! In reality, this life of idealism doesn't exist. What does exist is rest yet pain, calm yet chaos, life yet death, and joy yet stress. In these dichotomous experiences, our feelings begin to shape our perspective of life. Fortunately, feelings are not facts and perspectives can be reshaped.

Window to the Soul

I like to use the analogy that feelings are like a window to our soul. Imagine that you are on the outside looking in. I tend to describe feelings as what happens internall*y, what happens on the inside.* Emotions are similar to feelings but can be seen or observed on the outside, which can include feelings on the inside. These terms are quite interchangeable, and often used synonymously. Without developing insight as a parent, we may show a feeling of happy, sad, or mad, but not know what we are feeling or why. A feeling requires identification and is an opportunity to process and grow as a person. I believe our feelings reveal so much about us. While feelings are not facts, they are clues to help us see what we need. They can also show us what is being fulfilled in our lives. We feel worried because we think something bad might happen. We feel sad because something bad has happened. We feel happy because something good has happened.

Emotions are essential because they keep us connected with others and ourselves and reveal any needs we may have.

Each of our emotions is God-given and unique. Feelings are like fingerprints—there are patterns and similarities, but no two are identical. And thus, our feelings are the window pane through which we view our soul. What is your view of your soul? Is it full of hope or is it hurting? What feelings do you need to accept and process?

Feelings are life-giving, but can also be life-depriving. If our view remains on the window pane, focused on our feelings, we are missing out. Are you willing to go inside the house of your heart, where your true needs lie? I know for some right now, the very thought of owning our emotions and going to that place where emotions lead is terrifying. Breathe. I'm not asking you to do this alone. I believe and know that on the other side of our feelings is our freedom, so we must explore them in order to continue on our life's journey so we don't get stuck.

As we examine our feelings, we may experience both pain and joy. Emotions can reveal the deep wounds of betrayal and high peaks of intimacy and allow us to move forward into healing and growth. I love emotions because they keep us real. When we feel, we are alive. However, when we allow our feelings to control and consume us, we are of little good to our children and ourselves.

It may sound as if I'm playing both sides. Feelings are useful and essential, but we cannot let them lead us or be our endpoint. And this is the balance we must find—recognizing what we are feeling, yet having the insight to not be led by our feelings. We accomplish this when we determine the need that arises from a particular emotion and then focus on the need, not the feeling. It is possible to do this with positive and negative emotions. For example, when I feel an overwhelming sense of joy as I walk down the streets of a Disney park with my family and am caught up in tears of euphoria, I am satisfied as a mother. I often run too fast in life and spend too little time enjoying the family memories that I "work" so hard to make. That positive emotion I feel at the window of my soul during a Disney moment allows me to recognize the need I was filling at the time—the need of feeling fulfilled in motherhood. I can choose to recognize this and try to replicate satisfying that emotional need more often.

The same process works for negative emotions. If I am meeting with a child in foster care and she tells me a song reminds me of her mother, she expresses sadness and fear, which reveals a need in her soul that needs to be filled. As she expresses the song and how it makes her feel, I am able to see into her soul and know how I can help in her acceptance and healing process. She was feeling abandoned and unloved and was able to express it.

The window to our soul allows us to recognize a feeling. These feelings are clues to the deeper need. The next step is to ask, "Why am I feeling this?" and allow ourselves to work through the feeling to identify the corresponding need of the soul.

As you go through common emotions that parents experience, use this "window of the soul" visual to help you apply this process of examining the emotions that come up in your daily life. You can then help your children learn to do the same as they observe and listen to you. When children are small they have little awareness of their feelings and they learn about them through parents, peers, and caregivers. As children grow they experience many of the same feelings as an adult, but they lack the knowledge to recognize and identify what it is or to connect it to a need.

In general, Barney, the purple dinosaur, does a great job when he teaches preschoolers the difference between happy, mad, and sad. Happy means feeling good and joyful, it makes us smile. Sad feelings do not feel good, and they can make us cry and want to be alone. When we are mad, we are angry and want to yell or hurt someone. However, life is so complex that our feelings are often more than happy, mad, and sad. As we get older, we learn the complexities of life demand an emotional vocabulary that surpasses Barney's preschool songs. When our feelings seem bigger than we are, we tend to feel more than one at a time and cannot separate them easily. Feelings are harder to handle the more out of control of a situation appears.

Not having a large vocabulary list of feelings is a problem for adults too. If we don't know what is wrong, how can we fix it? When I met my husband, I knew he and I were different. Apart from being man and woman, he was an introvert and I was an extrovert. He said a hundred words a day; I spoke ten thousand. I was a feeler and he was, well, not a feeler. Josh was and is still such a balance to me. Because I feel in many ways, when I don't feel grounded, he grounds me. When we met, Josh had three emotions—and three is being generous. He was either happy, sad, or "eh." We later determined the "eh" feeling was melancholy. Now, nearly two decades later, Josh tells me he has four emotions, happy, sad, "eh," and a little anger sometimes. I will consider this progress. (The truth is, his feeling list is as extensive as mine, but his tendency toward efficiency in communication consolidates them into four general categories.)

You may feel like Josh. You may just have a basic set of three emotions and have never developed comprehensive feelings deeper than that. Still, our ability to identify what we feel is essential to insightful parenting. You may feel sad. Within feeling sad, there is usually a more specific feeling to identify: sullen, depressed, grief, lonely, rejected, tearful, heartbroken, humiliated. I have included a list of emotions and their more specific sub-feelings in appendix D for your development and use. Take some time to look through them to see how you can more specifically identify your emotions in a given situation. As you begin to identify your feelings and evaluate their roles in your parenting style and relationships, here are a few that are quite common to parents.

Anxiety

Anxiety arises from a sense of not knowing and trying to predict the unpredictable. It is fear of the future because of what has happened in the past. Anxiety shows itself in worry, fear, paranoia, hypervigilance, and helicopter parenting. This is a common response I see in many parents, especially mothers, and tends to be rooted in conscious or unconscious fear. We feel anxious when we sense something is out of our control. Whether past- or future-focused, we get stuck in the "I have no control" mindset. Whether real or imagined, we believe danger looms and so we feel anxious.

We tend to justify our anxiety as parents. We mask it as being "cautious or concerned." You can be cautious or concerned from a healthy place of logic and reason, but when concern becomes raw emotion and paranoia, this is anxiety. This can be better explained by examining it outside the complex parent-child relationship. Consider the *new car experience.* Have you ever had a new car? Ever ridden in your friend's new car? Been part of the new car discussion? Well, what is it usually about?

You experience pleasure, jubilee, and total enjoyment each time you enter that new car. Day after day, riding in the new car produces euphoric feelings of being blessed and enjoying the present moment. The car is treasured for what it is and simply enjoyed. If instead you focus on fear about new car, and are worried about getting it dirty, you'll never take it out to enjoy it. And even if you keep it in a garage, the new car smell will dissipate soon anyway, so being anxious about your new car keeps you from enjoying it. When we worry too much about tomorrow and the "what ifs" of life, we may say to ourselves, "This is stupid. I want to enjoy my car. I can't let tomorrow ruin my today. I'm going to enjoy my car." We cannot experience life through the lens of fear and anxiety.

When it's about a car, we can see this as clear fear and anxiety stealing our experiences of the new car. But we do this with our children and don't recognize it. We parent day after day. We parent our children from the day they are presented as a gift to us and into adulthood. Do we enjoy them as we do a new car? Do we wake up each day and see our children as a new experience and treasure to be enjoyed? Or do we worry so much about what might happen that we don't appreciate our time with them?

We allow our past to determine our future and rob us of the present. Rob us of our presents—our children. So, your challenge is to throw off the fear, recognize that your children are a gift that brings pleasure, jubilee, and total enjoyment in the experience. Yes, raising children is work (I'm not minimizing this), but when we have a new car, we don't obsess over maintenance, car washes, gas prices, etc. We enjoy the car and accept the work as part of the blessing. Well, enjoy your children today and accept the effort of discipline as part of the blessing. There is no seat for fear in a new car; nor should there be room for fear in our home as parents.

Guilt and Shame

Guilt and shame are conjoined twins that sabotage personal growth, relationships, and effective parenting. Guilt is the feeling that we have violated our own moral code and is internally focused. Shame is the feeling that others perceive us as bad and is externally focused on how we believe we are viewed by others. These feelings are amplified if we have a negative belief system or the wrong people on "the committee in our heads." Single mothers and fathers tend to experience guilt and shame a lot, as do surviving parents or divorced parents. The problem with living through a lens covered with shame and guilt is that we will never develop insightful parenting or a healthy view of ourselves or our children. We need to personally evaluate whether the expectations we have for ourselves as parents are realistic. If not, we are doomed to feel guilty, and the negative influences in our lives will gladly help us attach the stigma of shame to the seal the envelope. A single mother cannot also be the father to her children. She must accept what she is able to do, dismiss any unrealistic expectations, and create a new normal for herself and her children to help clean off guilt and shame from the window of her soul.

Hopelessness

Feeling hopeless is what sets in after we have experienced despair. Hopelessness is the feeling that we cannot change things and life will not get better. This is not a good emotion to harbor long-term. Hopelessness can, however, be a source of short-term motivation. For instance, when a mother feels she can no longer provide for her children, she may feel hopeless. But instead of sinking into depression and allowing the situation to grow worse, her despair motivates her toward change. She decides a move to a new city and a new school is the best thing she can do for herself and her children. This kind of action, using despair to spur us to a new outlook, turns hopelessness into hope. Hopeless is when we have given up hope. Hope looks forward. Hopelessness isn't looking anywhere. It is like emotional paralysis. When you find yourself feeling hopeless, reach out to your support system. If you don't have a support system, find a church or online support group. Many new and long-term parents experience a season of hopelessness when they realize life with children is different than they imagined. Perhaps adulthood is different than they imagined, and they just want to give up. Giving up is the last thing you and your children need. Just like every other feeling that obstructs our view of our soul, hopelessness tells you what you need, so you must step out and get it in order to move past this difficult emotion. Do you have a plan for getting out of hopelessness?

Anger

Anger is an emotion with two different roots. We may feel anger if we are hurt and not wanting to be vulnerable about the hurt, or we may be angry when we are unhappy with ourselves and refuse to deal with a problem. Many of these emotions are best evaluated and processed in the midst of a good self-care plan and coping skills. When you feel angry is the best time to stop and process. Do not react to a situation in anger. Anger clouds our judgment, and we are not effective communicators and therefore should not try to communicate when we are angry. Step away and process what you are feeling. Ask yourself if you feel angry about something your child did or is it about you? If your child angered you, why are you angry? By learning to identify the root of your anger, your children will learn to see anger as a clue to a deeper problem within themselves or with a situation. Once we see the problem, we then can identify whether to address it or let it go. Anger is a strong emotion, and like the others, a clue to a soul need such as acceptance, validation, or love. (Anger in these cases is not the righteous anger, i.e. passion, one may have about broad global issues, but rather a personal reaction to personal experiences.)

Feelings Thermometer

Another great tool I have created to help individuals process and regain control of their emotions is a "feelings thermometer" or "feelings scale." Thermometers are line-by-line calibrated to determine the measurement of a particular object or environment. We will use a "feelings thermometer" in our exercise. Often with feelings people tend to go from zero to ten without warning and without recognizing the changes that take place along the way. The truth is, we go through steps to get from zero to ten, and when we separate them and label them, we can see the progression of the emotion as it builds up. The feelings thermometer is a self-report of what changes you see and feel in yourself as a negative emotion builds up in you. (See appendix E, Feelings Thermometer.)

Here's an example of how I would use this exercise to gauge the level of anxiety in a teenager. Think of a related example in your own life where you can use the exercise to determine the "temperature" of your child's or your own emotion. Teen anxiety, especially in girls, often causes poor social skills, self-harm practices, isolation, and panic attacks. It is easy to get a teen to agree that peace, feeling calm, is the opposite of feeling anxious. As the teen imagines her thermometer, I have her label her negative emotion at the top of the scale. We then discuss and start with the number where she can most easily imagine its symptoms. Zero on the thermometer is the absence of the negative emotion and fullness of the positive. So, beside a zero on an anxiety scale, she may write, "I'm relaxed, happy, talking with friends and family. In a good mood." Then I ask, "When you begin to feel anxious, what is the first thing you notice about yourself?" This is usually a one and a mild change from zero. For a one on her thermometer, this teen may say, "I am still relaxed and happy but my eye begins to twitch and I am less talkative." I then ask what a two looks like and what a three looks like, and so on. I have her complete the steps that are easiest to imagine first, and then I have her fill in the gaps on the thermometer last. It is usually easiest to identify and label what a zero and ten look and feel like. Zero is no negative emotion and a ten is all of that emotion. In this case with the teenager, a ten is usually, "I have a panic attack, can't breathe, racing thoughts, isolated, sweating, scared." In separating these steps and identifying what a zero of anxiety looks like versus a ten, the teen can see the progression of an emotion, and she begins to feel a sense of control over a feeling she has not felt control over before.

As you reflect and create your own thermometer for different emotions, allow the steps to sink in. Process when you see a change in your behavior and when others notice the change in you. Ask yourself how you handle a feeling when it's a one versus a ten. Ask yourself what can help you regain control and at what number you need to be to address your feeling and still remain an insightful parent.

Not Being Changed

One saying I don't allow in my home is, "You made me..." as in "You made me mad, sad, or whatever." I have taught my children that they are in control of their feelings, and while experiences may trigger or create certain emotions, they can choose if they allow that feeling to remain or dismiss it. If our emotional responses to situations are learned from previous experiences, it is like building a tower of Legos; they stack on top of each other. When we face a new situation for the first time, the emotion we assign to it is influenced by similar life experiences in our past. Emotional responses are learned.

If I take a Popsicle from a baby, I have only taken a Popsicle. The baby may become upset, expressing an angry or confused emotion. However, if the baby learns that when someone takes a Popsicle, the baby gets a balloon, the baby may laugh when I take the Popsicle and feel joy and anticipation about receiving a balloon. The baby can learn that what might be a negative experience is actually positive. Experiences shape our emotional responses.

We must reclaim power over our feelings and not let our emotions lead our lives or be controlled by others. When I understand that I am in control of my emotions, and those outside of my physical body do not have power over my feelings, I can breathe deep in the freedom and power that I control how I respond. And when I do lose control of my feelings, I can recognize how to rein them in (see chapter 3) and learn from the experience to be better equipped for the stressor later.

I can honestly say, I feel a certain level of anxiety with some people. I can be enjoying a calm, mostly joy-filled day, but when I see particular people, my emotional balance gets sucker-punched. This is because I have identified this person as negative or a danger in some way. In these cases, I use my window to look into my soul and evaluate why I feel so uncomfortable with some people. Is it a past hurt? Or is this person not safe and my boundaries are not secure enough around them? I also use my Am Safe vs. Feel Safe exercise (see chapter 3 and appendix B) to deescalate my anxiety. I have determined some people just aren't safe, and I may never feel comfortable around them. But I don't let my feelings lead; I stay in control.

We never want to react with raw emotion; rather we seek to respond to situations and emotions with logic and reason. I now can recognize within myself, "I am feeling uncomfortable right now, but I am in control. My feelings will not lead me. I can be in this person's presence and not be changed." Strengthening your boundaries (as we discussed in chapter 4) and gaining personal insight improves this ability to maintain your composure.

Owning our feelings—tracing them to their roots and not letting others control our emotions—is easier said than done and easier typed than applied, but that doesn't change its truth. You and I are each in control of our own feelings, our own emotional thermometer, and can plan accordingly for those situations that have more power to influence our feelings than others. This book is cumulative and the information here can continue to build and grow in layers, developing further insights into your path to healing in order to be a more effective parent. Remember the benefit of healthy boundaries and the importance of establishing a support system of people who help you grow. Now reflect on who you can call upon to help process any negative feelings. Talk to your support person about those feelings, and consider professional counseling if you feel your issues are greater than your capacity to process them at this time.

Questions to Ponder

1. What emotions are visible in the window to your soul? What are they telling you?

2. Which emotions do you struggle with the most in your everyday life? Which are the most difficult in your parenting?

3. What steps can you take to improve the way you choose to control your emotions so they don't control you?

Activity

1. Using the Feelings Thermometer, appendix E, choose a negative emotion from this chapter that you deal with and write in your own thermometer readings so you can have it as a reference point when the emotion next arises.

2. Explore the list of feelings in appendix D and choose several main headings that apply to you, then read through the subheadings to determine the deeper feelings that may be causing a surface response. Write these in your journal.

3. Using your journal, write down the insight or insights from this chapter that you gained and how you can use them in your life and in your parenting.

PART 3
RESULTS

What motivates us to progress through difficult challenges? Positive results. The journey to insightful parenting is filled with struggles and pain, and that can sometimes lead to a desire to quit. Don't stop! You've made it so far in searching your inner self for the places where healing can occur. You now can look forward to the benefits resulting from your hard work. When you have taken the path toward wholeness, much of your life will reap the rewards. In particular, three results make all the effort worthwhile—hope, love, and healing.

Hope begins to replace despair and disappointment once you are able to move forward from past hurts and look forward to what is to come. Hope grows as we look to the future with a sense of anticipation in spite of life's circumstances. If you're moving away from the past struggles that have defined your present, your journey to a new destination will bring joy.

Love is what makes life worth living. But sometimes we've been so covered up by failure and hurt, we have a hard time giving and even receiving love. Freeing your soul from the hurts of the past allows you to love again, and to see love grow in healthy ways in all your relationships. Love helps us step outside of ourselves and enjoy the journey as people and as parents.

Healing is difficult, but the resulting sense of release and peace as we regain wholeness is worth it. When we commit to doing the hard work of self-development, we are on the path to healing. As we examine the places where healing is needed, and make a commitment to move through the pain to find a place of soul recovery, we bring healing not only to ourselves but to all the relationships with those we love.

One last benefit: as we learn to feel hope, love, and healing again, it will spill over into those around us, and our children will learn how to do the same, and be whole as the adults we desire them to become.

Chapter 7

Hope

Early on as a mother, I was overwhelmed and unable to keep up with all the expectations I had placed on myself. I feared I was failing myself and my family. I wasn't prepared for the disillusionment of adulthood and motherhood I was experiencing. I loved the *idea* of being a mother but the *experience* of being a mom came with sleepless nights, messy kitchens, and piles of laundry. While in the midst of my own despair, I saw the need for a strong support system. So, I reached out. I knew to find my inner hope I had to see hope in the making through other women who have gone before me in the journey of life.

One woman I looked to was my own mother. Amid conversation, early morning coffee, and a truck full of groceries, she gave me a nugget of hope. A nugget I could hold onto and live by. She told me that *spending time with my children is far more important than a clean house, folded laundry, or empty sink.* This simple truth gave me hope. It gave me permission to let go of trying to control too many things.

And I decided spending more time with my children would pay off for all of us.

What my mother taught me with a simple statement changed my perspective as a parent. I find similar truth in the Serenity Prayer by Reinhold Niebuhr.[3] The first stanza is commonly known, and often used in a shortened version with recovery groups. But so much truth is revealed and reinforced in the full original version. Intentionally read over it several times and let the words bring light into the dark places of your heart that need hope.

> God, give us grace to accept with serenity
> the things that cannot be changed,
> Courage to change the things
> which should be changed,
> and the Wisdom to distinguish
> the one from the other.

> Living one day at a time,
> Enjoying one moment at a time,
> Accepting hardship as a pathway to peace,
> Taking, as Jesus did,
> This sinful world as it is,
> Not as I would have it,
> Trusting that You will make all things right,

If I surrender to Your will,

So that I may be reasonably happy in this life,

And supremely happy with You forever in the next.

Amen.

—Reinhold

Neibuhr

When I was able to accept the things I had little power over and those I had no power over, I found hope. Hope starts with belief in a higher power that has your best interest at heart. It is the belief in a better outcome than what you can see in your current circumstance. It is the courage to take control and change your present to make a better future. Hope is a noun, verb, and adjective. It is that missing piece in your puzzle to finish the scene and continue your story.

Hope doesn't give up. Hope first starts with acceptance. Perhaps not full acceptance, but some acceptance of your current circumstances. Acceptance is not the same as endorsement; you may have some painful places you don't want to accept for fear that you are condoning the behavior or memories. Wrong. Acceptance is simply acknowledging that you do not have control to change a circumstance, especially if it is in the past. Acceptance is the ingredient necessary for hope to make its appearance. Forgiveness is an element of acceptance and necessary for hope to exist. If hope is the flower, forgiveness is the soil.

When I called my mom, and reached out for support as a new parent, I knew I had to accept the things I could not change and had to find a way to cope in the midst of this new season of life. I had much to be thankful for, but my expectations and perfectionism were depleting any semblance of joy I had and clouding my perspective of parenthood. After listening to my mom and deciding I had to get better for me and my family, I began to shift my perspective and priorities on a daily basis. By taking it one day at a time, the small victories were like flowers beginning to grow in my hope garden.

What about you? How has hope played a part in your story up to now? Do you have a garden full of hope flowers or do you need to process faulty perspectives and pull some weeds to make room for hope to grow?

You have more capacity for hope than you give yourself credit for. Too often, people see themselves as victims when they are far past that. A victim is only a victim when something is actively happening. Once an event is over, you are a survivor. For example, when I was prisoner to sleepless nights as a new mom, I was a victim during the night, but when the day came, I had survived the night. I knew dawn would bring a new opportunity for me and that gave me hope. Consider how far you have come in life. The courage, wisdom, and fortitude you have developed are all by-products of hope.

Even the slightest bit of hope still needs to be nurtured. The Serenity Prayer talks about taking it one day at a time and enjoying each moment as it comes. We lose the opportunity for hope in our lives when we move too fast or get stuck in the quicksand of life's negative events. Too often we don't stop in the midst of hope moments to let the seed take root and let one more flower blossom in our hope garden.

Hope is a Choice

Can you look back and see the hope garden you have built throughout the years? Hope builds on hope. Perhaps after your first sports competition as a child, your team may have lost but your coach encouraged you so much that the loss mattered less than the love you felt from your coach. You chose hope. Or perhaps you witnessed your parents' divorce and thought you might never see happy parents again, but the precious time you were able to spend with them one-on-one filled you with joy and you knew it would be okay. You chose hope. Maybe you have lost a child or parent to an unfortunate situation. In the pain and devastation, you decided something needed to be done to combat the sickness and cancer that took your loved one. You became an advocate for such a cause. You chose hope.

Life without hope is full of despair, disillusionment, and disappointment. But a life with hope presses through the negative and seeks to find a purpose or use for everything. Hope discovers where you can make a difference and does just that. While some of the hardest moments in life can never be explained or justified, they can be used. Hope uses the pain to find purpose and uses the loss to find love.

Hope is what you find after all the dust and grief has settled and you find peace. It is like a parent who lost her son. For years she was stuck in despair. When she pictured her family carrying on in the journey of life, she saw her son behind them, and she couldn't help but turn around and become fixated on her son, still there, stuck in the past. And so, she too stayed stuck in the past, wishing circumstances were different. One day after years of grieving, she began to picture her family again, and she noticed her son was not behind them anymore; he was ahead of them, awaiting them in the future. She realized she had accepted she could not change the past, but knew she had a future in eternity that she could spend with her son. She found hope.

Hope is Light

Dr. Martin Luther King once said, "Darkness cannot drive out darkness; only light can do that. Hate cannot drive out hate;

only love can do that." Hope is light. Hope is a choice. Like a cool spring breeze, it sits at the window waiting to be let in. Imagine the window to your soul right now. Does hope need to be let in?

As a parent, you have been working so hard to give your children the best life possible, but have you given them the gift of hope yet? We cannot give what we don't have. You must have hope to give it. We must believe something for it to be real in our lives. Our children will believe what we believe, good or bad. They will look at our motives, our mindsets, and our actions, and will model after us. If we find hope in hopeless situations, they will. If we find purpose in despair, they will. These are our opportunities to build a generation of victors and survivors. Accept hope for yourself and let your children see what it can do. Hope changes things.

Hope is essential to insightful parenting. It helps you accept life for what it is and begin to take charge of your life regardless of circumstances. Hope is the precise balance between relinquishing control of the things you are powerless over and accepting control over the things you can control. Do you know what you can control? Yourself. Your attitude. When your children begin to see you making choices that build you up, choices that are made out of hope and not despair, they will mirror these behaviors. Our children will see and then experience hope for themselves.

Hope Shatters Negative Thinking

When we are stuck it is difficult to will ourselves out of a mindset of negativity. That is why I told you about my mother. When we are stuck in a hole, we may need a ladder or a rope sent in from someone on the outside. This is where your support system, self-care plan, and positive thinking all come into play. By surrounding yourself with positive people and healthy behaviors, you can reduce the negative thinking and regain hope.

When we are used to being negative we will remain negative; when we want to be positive we must choose positive. Have you ever stopped to listen to the tapes playing in your head? We all have them. They are constant internal messages that dictate how we handle situations. If we live life feeling defeated, we likely have tapes playing that tell us we are worthless and only deserve the worst in life. If we live life feeling confident, we likely have tapes playing that tell us we can achieve great things and can handle tough situation.

Listen closely to the tapes in your head. If they are lying to you, they need to be replaced. You are what you think you are and can become what you think you can become. Hope can pave the way to positive parenting experiences. It can pave the way to loving yourself for who you were made to be. Hope heals the broken places and replaces the negative tapes in our head. Our work begins when we notice these negative tapes about ourselves and the messages we have believed about situations and begin to replace them. So much of life is changed through the perspective we have.

Hope Grants Grace

Maybe you had hope and lost it. Maybe you were once a positive person and something changed that. The beauty of hope and the Serenity Prayer is that is doesn't matter what you were before; hope says a new opportunity is available today. I get it—sometimes as parents we feel we have messed up too much. This is a lie. We feel we are too old to change. This is a lie. We feel our life has had so much bad happen that we can't find hope. This is a lie. Give yourself permission to fail and accept that hope is ready for you whenever you are. Give yourself grace to grow in hope, regardless of whether failure comes. Failure is only failure if we don't learn from our mistakes.

Hope is as much a journey as life itself. The hope I needed as a new mother wasn't enough hope later when I was getting my second degree, nearing bankruptcy, and watching my parents' divorce. The further we get in life, the more complex our circumstances become, and thus the more hope we need. When life is good, then hope helps paints the sky bright colors. When life is bad, hope helps keep us out of the deepest parts of the pit.

We must remember to give ourselves grace for hope to grow and accept that it will look different in different seasons of life.

Hope Forgives

Hope is always available and always forgives. Forgiveness accepts that the past is in the past and you choose to look forward to the future. This is hope in action. However, at times we may just be too tired to choose hope and forgiveness. We pull the covers over our head and sleep a little while longer. That is okay, but when you wake, choose hope. The more you choose hope, you will see hope has been choosing you all along. Hope is an endless resource and always available whether we access it or not. We are only human and will fail. When we do, we need to forgive ourselves and start the day new. Hope learns from the past to make for a better future.

Source of Hope

What is your source of hope? Perhaps it is the wisdom from your grandmother that you remember as a child. Perhaps it is the rhythmic cycle of the sun, knowing each day is a new opportunity. For me, my hope is rooted in a biblical verse that compels me to know things will be okay, despite how it may seem at the time: "And we know that in all things God works for the good of those who love him, who have been called according to his purpose."

Finding a source of hope is essential; no one is made to do life alone. We need a source of hope greater than ourselves. Having our hope rooted in something bigger than us allows us to know that when we reach our end of hope, there is still more available because the source is endless. Maintaining access to your source of hope helps you remain full of hope, reminding you that you are never alone and aren't living life solo. Hope is always with you, if you chose to find it.

Hope Builds Resilience

Chances are, you have lived long enough to know life is not perfect and cannot be controlled. You can also know that through hope you can survive anything and nothing has the power to destroy your spirit. The window to your soul can be opened and a fresh breeze of hope can fill your soul and better equip you from one experience to prepare you for the next. Hope doesn't let our lives go to waste. It uses the good, bad, and ugly to take us to the next step of being a better parent and person. Hope makes us resilient because we are able to look back at all we have endured and overcome, and helped others overcome, and see how it equips us for future experiences. Your resilience will help your children be resilient. As parents we want so much to prevent our kids from experiencing the difficult things in life, but the truth is, we cannot control that. What we can control are tools like hope and resilience, so that our children can learn to use these tools when tough times come. This is insightful and successful parenting.

Questions to Ponder

1. In what areas of your life can you apply the Serenity Prayer? How will it make a difference in your attitude and responses?

2. How can you learn to "accept" more of what you cannot change?

3. Are you generally a hopeful person or do you struggle with hopelessness? How has either of these approaches affected your life and relationships?

4. Do you believe in the power of hope? Where can you use more hope in your life?

Activity

1. In your journal, write down the insight or insights you've gained from this chapter and how you can apply them to your life and your parenting.

2. Write out the Serenity Prayer in your journal and personalize it to your life's circumstances.

Chapter 8

Love

Love is a verb and a noun. It is an ingredient and an outcome of insightful parenting. Love is at the root of insightful parenting. It is selfless. Love is secure in where it stands and therefore can give without fear of what may be reciprocated (or unreciprocated). As you continue to work on yourself, remember it is not selfish to want to be healthy. It is an act of love. When you love yourself and understand the value of giving love and being loved, you then can pass that same gift to your children.

Like hope, love must be defined, experienced, nurtured, and then given. There are usually two camps of people when it comes to love: Those who have experienced love and understand it, and those who have not experienced love and do not understand it. I say only two camps, because love, though it requires relationship, can be between you and yourself. It can be between you and God—which is where I believe it needs to start. Like hope, we need to have a clear understanding that we are loved from a power greater than ourselves and that we are worth being loved by such a great power. Once we see our value through the lens of love, we begin the journey of healing. To some extent, you already know that you are of value because you are dedicating time to becoming more insightful about yourself and, in turn, your children.

We have to be willing to see love when it comes. We will develop and recognize some truths about love in the following pages, but first I want to share a story about where I found love. One Christmas, my children were so excited about their gifts for us that they couldn't wait until Christmas day. My daughter kept telling me, "You don't have it yet, but you will use it every day." When her gift was ready, just after Thanksgiving, she asked me to sit on the couch. The first thing I opened was her handmade note, which read, "I hope you use and wear this every day." I was excited. She had a big smile on her face. The first gift was a beautiful filigree broach from her school's Christmas boutique. I loved it. The second gift was a handmade clay espresso cup. I loved it. What I appreciated even more is that I saw that my daughter understands love. At ten years old, she was able to think about what I like and find gifts that reflected my interests and that I could use often. Love is the consideration of others before yourself. But as we will learn, love can only be given if you first have it for yourself.

When love is only a feeling—and as we know, feelings change with the wind—love runs the risk of disappearing. Love must be a conscious, intentional choice, not based on a feeling and not changing. What love looks like may change, how love feels may fade, but love itself has to be stable. It has to be a commitment to bettering oneself and others in our circle of influence. Sometimes love is waking in the middle of the night and feeding an infant. It may be lying on the bathroom floor with a sick child. Or it may simply be you taking a trip to your special place for a moment and giving yourself time to reset and recharge.

Love Must be Defined

Few things in life can be achieved if we do not first take time to understand them. We cannot build a house without knowing how it is constructed. We cannot win a baseball game if we don't know how to swing a bat or throw a ball. And you cannot love if you do not understand it from a healthy perspective. While the dictionaries define *love* as deep affection, endearment, fondness, intimacy, and attachment to someone or something, love is so much more. Genuine, insightful love, that will help you as a parent and in life, should not be confined to a feeling. In fact, sometimes love has to be a choice we make in spite of how we feel.

Love can be examined from two perspectives: need and pleasure. Need-based love is the love a child needs from its parent. An infant can suffer with failure to thrive without physical touch, affection, and nurturing. These acts of love toward the infant are necessary and therefore based in part on the need of the child. The child is not being selfish when crying over a dirty diaper, or its inability to self sooth. The child needs to be physically cared for in order to survive, in order to know it is loved.

Pleasure-based loves are well defined by author C. S. Lewis. In his book *The Four Loves*, he defined empathy, friend, erotic, and unconditional "God" love as what people experience in a lifetime.[5] The four loves are fluid, and people can experience one or another or multiple types in their lives, often simultaneously. A love of a spouse can fulfill both the friend and erotic love if the relationship is healthy. Different loves are fulfilled through the bonds between you and other people, and not all of our relationships will be defined by the same types of love. Each love fills and satisfies a different part of our soul.

These categories by Lewis can be a good way to evaluate your soul, especially in the areas of empathy, friendship, and feeling accepted by God. All the loves are based in appropriate expression and reciprocation when in a healthy relationship.

True love is given without expecting something in return, including when it feels unreciprocated. When you are confident in the love you give, you give it freely. For instance, a parent whose child struggles with drug addiction may choose to continue to love and invite their child over to dinner in spite of the lack of reciprocation of love from the child.

In a mutually healthy relationship, you will also be open enough to discuss when it seems love is lacking or behaviors are unloving. Love is respectful but it also corrects. Therefore, children *can* be disciplined in love and should *only* be disciplined in love. Remember to ask yourself if the discipline is about you or the child. Love helps you take the pause to make that determination as an insightful parent. Love asks, "Will this help or harm?"

Love Must be Experienced

These definitions of love help paint a picture of what it looks like and hopefully help you recall positive memories you have of love—how it feels, acts, and looks. Our adult definitions of love often stem from the experiences we had with love earlier in life. Perhaps as a child you saw your parents, in the midst of financial struggles and emotional hardships, still make time for family dinners at the local pizzeria. Or perhaps your single mother worked two jobs to provide for you and your siblings. Love requires sacrifice and sometimes requires that we take a different perspective. The child whose parents struggled financially can choose to remember the value placed on family meal time as an act of love. For the child of the single mother, love looked like the sacrifice of family time so that bills could be paid. Both choices are sacrifice through love.

Love may not look the same to all of us, but the intention is always the same with love. A decision made in love is made from a tender place in your heart that serves to help and build up the other person. When you receive love, you experience being valued. When you give love, you are showing value to your loved ones.

If love has been lacking in your past, you may have to be more intentional and deliberate in your understanding and expression of love, because it doesn't come naturally. How have you experienced love in your life? Is it through loving your children? Do you remember having a deep inner feeling of joy, satisfaction, and affection toward them or your significant other? Maybe you remember receiving love from your parent or grandparent, or even a friend or teacher at school, if you didn't experience it at home. Recalling the moments of love in your life gives you examples to replicate and pass on to your children. If family meals made you feel special, then have family meals. If taking a walk in the rain made you feel loved, then let your kids play in the rain. When we stop, look, and listen to the needs of our children, we can learn what they need to feel loved. And when we stop, look, and listen within ourselves, we can see what will help us know that we are loved.

Love Must be Nurtured

Love is like a flower—in the right environment (the right soil, water, and sun) it can grow with little effort. Realistically, in our world today, while every environment needs love, not every environment nurtures love. Therefore, nurturing love must be intentional. When you define love and know what it takes to love, and then listen to how others need to be loved, you can then know the right combination of soil, water, and sun to help their love flower grow. Gary Chapman has developed a wonderful test for learning how best to communicate love to one another. His book *The Five Love Languages* explains the five ways people give and receive love. Learning that love is a form of communication (verb) and also something to be communicated (noun) shows us it can be studied, learned, and understood.

The five love languages Dr. Chapman discusses are quality time, acts of service, words of affirmation, physical touch, and gifts.[6] Given what we've learned about healthy relationships, we know that when we are in a relationship with someone, that relationship should be mutually beneficial. While love gives without expecting in return, a healthy relationship reciprocates love for love, though it may be in different ways. When we give or receive love, it tends to be through the five methods mentioned above.

If your love language is quality time, then you feel loved when someone spends time with you. If your love language is acts of service, then you experience love through having your spouse or children do chores around the house. These examples help you begin to determine how you might best receive love. When we tend to give love in the same way we receive it, this is where love can be lost in translation. If my love language is quality time but my husband's is words of affirmation, sitting on the couch together means less to him than it does to me, while paying me a compliment may mean less to me than it does to him. As the saying goes, when in Rome do as the Romans; when you are in relationship, learn the love language of the other party and speak in that way to them, and let them know your love language so they can talk to you.

Self-Examine

We love from our soul. Love comes from within. Our ability to speak the language of love is contingent on how we love ourselves. As you begin to digest what love is and how it can be developed, be sure you are practicing grace with yourself. Grace is the combination of love and forgiveness, accepting that you may not always get it right. Simply recognizing that you are only human, and remembering to keep your personal expectations—and expectations in any relationship—realistic will help love grow. Remember that apologizing when you have not acted out of love goes a long way. Your children will learn from your willingness to accept yourself, flaws and all.

In previous generations parents did not apologize to their children. Instead, they had a "do as I say and not as I do" mindset and a "because I said so" attitude. This did not help to cultivate a mutual language of love for children to follow. When I became a parent, I decided I wanted my children to know that when I lost my cool, I was wrong and needed to ask for their forgiveness. By modeling humility and being able to admit I make mistakes, my children have learned how to give and ask for forgiveness. By my own self-examination and examining the patterns of families around me, I was able to determine that sometimes the best way to love my children is to be willing to say, "I'm sorry."

A positive result of self-examination and developing insight is that we can recognize how crisis and expectations affect how we give and receive love. We know that when we have experienced crisis, our ability to see into our soul and give and receive from a healthy place is restricted and clouded by a misguided perspective. Consider how crisis has changed your opinion and experiences of love. What have you learned about love from the crises in your life? When we experience crisis and begin to work through it, addressing the changes it has caused in our lives, the process changes us, and our appreciation for love becomes greater. We have a deeper understanding of the value, cost, and sacrifice of love.

Love is a Verb

When we consider how to act in love, we can turn to an idealistic measure and set the bar high. It is like they say: Shoot for the moon and you will land among the stars. While idealism can be paralyzing, it can also be motivating. I believe when you are training for anything, you must aim high, so that even if you don't reach your high goal, your efforts still produce good results. When training for a race, we run to win. When studying for a test, we study for an A. And when we are practicing love, we practice with that same level of intention. The Bible says, "Love is patient, love is kind. It does not envy, it does not boast, it is not proud. It does not dishonor others, it is not self-seeking, it is not easily angered, it keeps no record of wrongs. Love does not delight in evil but rejoices with the truth. It always protects, always trusts, always hopes, always perseveres. Love never fails."[7]

Love in action in a family is hard at times. Using the filter of "love" when making decisions can still leave parents with a lot of questions. Do we disagree in front of the children? Should the children help us make decisions about vacations? Can our children decide what is for dinner? For some questions, in your family the answer is an obvious yes or no. If, however, there are unhealthy patterns of communication in your family, then love may not be present regardless of the answer to any of these questions. These are points for you and your family to ponder. The answers to these questions are dependent on your individual and family's emotional and mental health.

One thing I see improving from previous generations is that parents are giving more respect to their children and allowing them to participate in family decisions. While we need to be careful not to give our children too much power, they need to feel loved and a contributing part of the family. Yes, let children weigh in on vacations, but parents you make the final decision. And the same goes for dinner.

Now the greater and more difficult display of love: communication. A pattern I see in previous generations is how parents argued. Parents would only have "discussions" (i.e. arguments) behind closed doors, or the families who were public about their disagreements would yell and scream. These two extremes do not offer a healthy role model for new parents to follow. As parents we have the opportunity for our children to see, hear, and learn healthy communication from us, including the fact that two people who love each other can have a disagreement, and not yell, scream, or curse. If we do not teach and model healthy, loving communication, our children's example may be political debates or prime-time television.

These are not "healthy" love examples. If we never disagree in front of our children, they never learn the art of communication and healthy discussion. But if we yell, scream, and use profanity, they feel unsafe, and this is actually a form of abuse.

The Golden Rule

When I was young there was a poster in one of my school classes—The 50 things I Learned in Kindergarten. One line in particular is universal for healthy relationships and interactions: *Do unto others as you would have them do unto you.* I didn't realize then how powerful this statement truly is. It isn't only about external interactions toward other people; it starts within us. How do we treat ourselves? This is applicable to communication, relationships, love, and insightful parenting.

While I know I am not the perfect picture of love, I like to believe I can be *love in action* to my children. I can display love toward others, knowing that I desire love myself. This is where knowing our value is significant in learning to love others, because to genuinely love others, we must first love ourselves. We cannot give what we do not have. Through our actions our children learn to love themselves and then love others.

When love is present, there is no room for doubt, fear, anxiety, or despair. True, authentic, deep love breaks through the clouds and sheds light into the darkness. Love brings peace into the storm. When in the midst of crisis, love can be found in the eye of the storm. It is the messenger of hope for the hopeless. Love and hope are like peas in a pod and essential ingredients to healing. Love isn't the great equalizer; it is the great neutralizer. It neutralizes because it brings you into the state of feeling calm, cool, and collected. Think on your self-care practices; they work because you are inserting love, peace, and all that is good into all that feels bad. Love is your secret weapon. Love perseveres in the face of adversity. When it seems as if you can't go another day without your teenager talking to you, love gets you through. You make that choice. Knowing you can't fight fire with fire, love is water for the fire that may be brewing in your home.

Love is Resilient

Love makes us resilient. Resilience is the ability to bounce back in the face of adversity, the ability to recover when experiencing resistance. Whether you are bouncing back or withstanding adversity, love can be your protective layer. When you love yourself and grow in accepting yourself for who you are, you become resistant to the attacks against you by others. I once heard it said that as parents, we need to fill up our kids with so much love that when the world pokes holes in their glass, they won't run out of water. Love is the water that keeps our children filled. How can you fill up your child today? How do you need to be filled up today?

When we believe in ourselves and model being resilient against the negative of the world, our children learn it. One of my favorite songs for my daughter is by the artist Plumb, "In My Arms." The song paints a word picture of storms, rain, and crashing waves, displaying how life will get hard for our little ones. Then she sings in the chorus about the child being safe in the mother's arms. Though it breaks my heart that I can't stop the storms of life, I want my children to be safe in my arms. While I can predict and diffuse some storms, I know I can't shelter my children from everything. I want to teach my children resilient love and be a source of replenishing love for them when these times come. I want them to know they can run to me and will be safe in my arms. This replenishing love will help them learn resilience.

Love is being in the arms of one who loves and protects you. Resilience doesn't say there won't be adversity; it says we will be able to stand after an adverse situation, like a crisis or major life event.

Still a Struggle

Perhaps love is still a struggle for you. Perhaps there is still too much hurt, pain, or shame in the way. The activities and questions to ponder in the earlier chapters will help you address these feelings. As you become healthier as a person, you also gain insight to love and what it looks and feels like. You learn how love can remain even in the absence of emotion. Love is a choice. It is totally acceptable to go back and forth in feeling that you have a handle on knowing how to give and receive love. In fact, being aware of your struggle in this area is a sign that you are practicing insightful parenting. When you stop to listen to your own feelings and recognize how they may get in the way of loving your children, you practice a healthy pause. You are learning to respond instead of react.

If you want to dig deeper but feel it has just been too long or there is too much pain for you to experience or give love, I want to encourage you to seek out and read *Abba's Child* by Brennan Manning.[8] When I was struggling to heal, I first needed to feel deep love. I found the experience of deep love in the midst of the pages of Manning's book. Learning that my value and identity were not tied up in my works or anything in this world helped me understand that love is so closely connected to faith and hope, it is difficult to genuinely experience one without the other.

Faith, Hope, and Love

When there is mention of faith, hope, and love, people tend to trivialize them, or dismiss them as legitimate tools toward a healthy living plan and seek them only as "last resort" fixes for problems. We have to remember, if something can help us get out of a crisis, it can keep us out of a crisis. Knowing that we are mind, body, and spirit beings, we have to seek wellness in all areas. As mentioned earlier, faith is both a coping tool and a source of strength. Hope is the thinking that keeps us future focused while appreciating the present. And love is the noun and verb that can help our relationships flourish. We must be intentional to make faith, hope, and love a part of our lives. They are essential ingredients to remember as we move on in the journey toward insightful parenting.

Questions to Ponder

1. Which aspects of love in this chapter were new to your understanding of love?

2. How can you experience love as both a noun and a verb in your present relationships?

3. In which areas of your life or which relationships do you need to apply more love? How can you do this?

4. Which of the four types of love are you experiencing in your life? What voids need to be addressed?

5. How can you give yourself more love?

Activities:

1. Write down your love language and those of the people closest to you. Write down ways you can express love to them in their language even if it is not your own. (Read *The Five Love Languages* by Gary Chapman if you need more help with this.)

2. Spend some time journaling and evaluate the individuals in your life. What loves are being fulfilled in your life? What types of love are you experiencing in your relationships? Are there fulfillments or voids that need to be addressed?

3. Write down in your journal the insight or insights you've had in this chapter and how you can apply them to your life and your parenting.

Chapter 9

Healing

What comes to mind when you think of the word *healing*? A scar on your arm? A wound in your heart? Perhaps a past memory? Simply stated, healing is being better today than you were yesterday. Healing is improvement. Like every other process and concept mentioned so far, it is not a steady growth experience. When we grow, we might regress, then grow more, and maybe regress a little bit again. Perhaps the saying "one step forward, two steps back" originally referred to the healing process. However, do not be discouraged if there seems to be no end in sight. The further you get in your healing process, the less regression you'll experience.

Take a moment and reflect on your current life circumstances. How do you perceive them? How can healing improve them? Whether mental, emotional, or physical, I believe every situation in life has room for growth and improvement. Think about where you were when you began this book. You may not have recognized it at the time, but you were already on your healing journey. Begin to recall the progress you have made already, about your thoughts, boundaries, perceptions, emotions, and insights. How have hope and love built upon this knowledge? All the concepts we've explored thus far are integral aspects of healing, and each new insight you receive contributes to the healing process.

Healing is a long-term process because it is a constant growth and development of you as an individual. It is the lifelong journey of recovering the parts of you that may have been lost or damaged and creating a new masterpiece—a masterpiece that would never had existed had you not recovered the painful parts of your past. Conversely, people sometimes talk about temporary healing. This is a short-term coping skill that helps you get through a situation, but does not replace the need of the long-term healing process. Sometimes we just need a quick 1-2-3 process to get ourselves settled (calm, grounded) in a situation if we feel overwhelmed. This is short-term coping; it is like a Band-Aid to stop the bleeding until you can address the wound later.

Short-Term Coping

An immediate remedy can stabilize us when we feel we are losing control and may have been triggered by something. This strategy for immediate composure is necessary when a parent is triggered by something in the past, but at the moment is unable to retreat in order to address the root of the hurt. Sometimes parents don't have the luxury to go visit the therapist in the midst of dinnertime, homework assignments, and baths (or at least the thought of a bath every night) when a word or behavior rises up to cause pain.

It is no secret parenting is hard. The question is, are you up for it? If you can learn to put aside that present hurt and be willing to seek immediate, though temporary, healing in those moments, then you are saying yes. Yes, to knowing when you need a time out. Yes, to knowing when it's time for some music. Yes, to saying you are sorry when you blow your top. The best way to deal with hurt in the everyday moments is to learn to bandage your wound before you react to your child.

Because I am intentional in ensuring everything I share with you I have implemented myself, I feel it was divine appointment that the week before I wrote this chapter, I found myself overwhelmed with routine needs of afterschool responsibilities. As my kids were displaying typical childlike behaviors, I found myself feeling a sense of failure, resentment, and frustration as the stress level rose. In that moment I identified the need for a temporary Band-Aid. It was my responsibility as a mother to first focus on my ability to control myself and not let my actions negatively impact my children. I knew if I did not patch my wound, it would result in further hurt and pain for all parties.

During times of stress, we as parents are more sensitive and tend to react rather than respond. It is important to remember feelings are neither good nor bad; how we respond to what we feel produces either a positive or negative outcome for us and our loved ones. This is an integral element in gaining insight. We recognize what we feel and pause to internally process or temporarily excuse ourselves from a situation so that we respond to our children according to what they need, not what we need. In this chapter, we're going to learn a step-by-step process for short-term coping. I will coach you through a short worksheet below, where you can take five minutes to ask yourself the questions that will help you better understand yourself and in turn better understand your child. This worksheet will help you understand the resilience that you have as a parent and help your child gain the insights you learn along the way.

How was this task for you? There is personal validation when you take a moment to step away, recognize what is happening within you, and consciously decide to address the issue later. The benefit to keeping the worksheet short is also a conscious effort on your part to not give too much time or attention to a matter when circumstances dictate otherwise. If

your children are in need and the rice needs to be s
perhaps it's not the right time to take thirty minutes to address
the wound in your soul you know is there. Our children will see
our resilience in our ability to maintain composure over our
feelings in necessary situations. And they will see our resilience
in addressing these emotions and wounds at the proper times
through the lifelong process of healing.

In your journal, answer the following questions. Remember,
this activity is like a visit to the clinic. You find the wound,
clean it up, put a bandage on it, and then go to the doctor later.
This is to get you grounded and stable to resume what you were
doing before you became overwhelmed with negative emotion.

1. Describe what happened. (max. three sentences)

2. Identify what you are feeling? (max, three feelings)

3. What were you doing when you were triggered and how
   can you return to the task appropriately?

4. What emotion and mindset is most appropriate for this
   task?

5. Breathe, compose yourself, and return to the task.

Healing as a Lifelong Process

The short-term coping activity is a useful tool to bandage our hurts until we have time to address our wound, or to handle those quick momentary hurts that arise. Addressing our wounds happens in the lifelong process of healing. Remember, wounds are the painful parts of our soul that need our attention in order for us to be insightful parents. As you know by now, everything about how you respond to your children first starts with what is happening within you. Lifelong healing is comprehensive and builds on itself. It is like math class, where the tools and formulas you learn early on are essential for you to complete later, more complex tasks. I intentionally placed hope and love right before this chapter because they are essential ingredients to healing. Love and hope propel us to be better individuals and learn to heal as well as pay forward the grace we have been given. Hope and love are also the life rafts we can hold on to when we feel we are drowning in the chaotic waves of life.

When I began my healing journey, it was nothing as organized as the chapters in this book. I didn't have the knowledge, tools, or confidence to proceed with caution into unchartered territory. While many of my adulthood issues stemmed from childhood experiences, I spent twenty years keeping a Band-Aid on an open wound that was begging to be tended to. As I began the healing journey, I once again relied on my faith, and I received three words that have stuck with me to this day. *Faith. Endure. Time.*

Letting these words sink in, I processed each one:

- I needed to have *faith* that things would get better and work out in the end.
- I would need to *endure* the journey, especially the pain along the healing process.
- It would take *time* for me to be well.

I have believed in and held to these truths through the years, and they have carried me a long way. When I decided to take off the Band-Aid off and address the wounds of my life, I made sure I had a support system of people around me who could shine a light on the path when I felt I had lost my way. These people did not replace my faith in God, but supported me on the healing path he led me down.

Faith

What has your journey looked like thus far? Do you have a light shining in front of you? Can you see where you have been? Do you believe that no matter how difficult your current situation, it can be part of your story in the future in a positive way? Do you trust that today is no accident and neither is tomorrow? Faith is essential in our healing because we have to believe we are more than just happenstance creations. If we were mere accidents, what is the reason for using what happened yesterday to make a better day for ourselves today and in the future? Faith says *you are in the exact season you need to be for the exact reason you need to be in the exact time you need to be*. When we use this perspective to look back at a past hurt and can find a purpose in the midst of the painful places to carry into the present, we can begin to heal. A healed parent makes for a healthy child.

Endure

This isn't a pretty word. It signifies struggle, adversity, doubt, and trouble. Remember our chapters about relationships, family, and feelings? And the negative memories that may have come up? Were you able to gain some insight about yourself throughout the chapters? If so, you chose to endure. It isn't easy to look into our souls or address our past hurts, but you chose to do so. When it comes to healing after hurting, we must endure to get to the other side. There is quite a difference in talking about our willingness to endure and actually pressing on in spite of difficulty.

Think about athletes training for the Olympics. Just as the gold medal is at the end of an arduous journey of commitment and exercise, your victory of healing and wellness is at the end of honest and authentic time with yourself. The real question for someone seeking insight in the midst of healing is: Am I willing to endure?

Time

They say time heals all wounds. I don't know about that, but I do believe time is an asset for the insightful parent. Time often brings a clearer perspective. How long has it been since you made the decision to get well? To become insightful? How long have you been hurting or had too small of a bandage on too big of a wound? Time will use all of this. Remember, the Band-Aid is part of the healing process. Take a minute now to reflect on it all. The moments you have taken to compose yourself, correct your thinking, and make peace with your past all play a part in your life story. This story is being lived by you now and will be carried on the wings of time through generations as your children reflect your growth and learn the resilience of hope and love in spite of adversity.

Time must be respected because it is constantly diminishing. Once a moment is gone, it is no longer here. This is helpful for survivors of abuse, to remember that the past is in the past. Time is also motivation for parents to take the steps toward insight now, and be that healthy parent for your children today instead of waiting for tomorrow. Time is arguably the st essential element to insightful parenting. Time is the difference between reacting and responding. Time will tell you if your reaction is about you or your child. Time gives you the opportunity to sit alone with yourself to ask the deep questions and go to the difficult places. Time helps to heal, because when you allow time to let the waves of life settle, or at least your emotions, you are able to consider a situation and decide what is best from an objective place and not in the rush of the moment.

Triangles

While faith, endure, and time are essential elements, other triangles or "threes" are useful in the journey of healing. In his book *Changes that Heal*, Dr. Henry Cloud uses grace, truth, and time as core elements to the healing process.[9] We have talked about these three throughout the book and their significance in insightful parenting. In addition to Dr. Cloud, a foundational technique in the therapy world is cognitive-behavioral therapy (CBT). CBT is rooted in the cognitive triangle that says our thoughts affect our feelings, which in turn affect our beliefs. The way we think, feel, and behave are directly related to one another. When we change one (thinking), we influence the others to change (feelings, behaviors). And when we consistently change one, we will inevitably change the others.

For example, I once worked with a woman who was suffering from depressive disorder and anxiety. Although she had not experienced any direct or secondary trauma, she was afraid to go outside and had no hope in life. Her thinking was the result of learning from her mother, who was much the same way. It was a generational pattern. I assigned her to begin and end each day writing something she was thankful for on her wall calendar. Also, we discussed the tapes that played in her head like, "Something bad will happen" and "I have nothing to live for." We challenged the truths behind these tapes. She began to recognize there was no truth behind the tapes—they were just tapes—and then she began to see something good in each day by writing it on her calendar. Slowly her depression began to lift and her anxieties lessened. She was willing to endure the process, which took months, but pressed into her thoughts, challenged her thinking, and changed her behaviors. Through persistence and effort, she recognized that thoughts are not always facts. She challenged her own faulty thinking, which resulted in positive lasting effects.

The cognitive triangle is timeless and used in many different sectors. Christian books use it to help someone deepen their faith. Doctors use it to help surgery patients and cancer survivors heal and recover. Coaches use it to get their athletes to perform with excellence. Even teachers use it to help students succeed on exams. As parents, the cognitive triangle is a tool not only for our own healing but also for helping your children develop personal insight.

Let Healing Continue

I hope so far in this journey you are pleased with the progress. That you are feeling stronger and seeing a healthier you than before you began the book. The healing process will continue from here. And may even continue forever. We may heal from different wounds, but as we grow, there may always be an offence or a harsh word requiring us to revisit these tools.

So far, we have discovered the value of learning to appreciate the journey more than the destination. We know that insight is key to healthy parenting, and comes through evaluating our relationships, our family, and our feelings. Then we built upon these through accepting hope and love as key ingredients in the healing process. Going forward, I want to build you up. It is time for you to know who you are, the value you have, and the legacy you will leave.

Questions to Ponder

1. What is the benefit of understanding that healing is both temporary and lifelong?

2. How have you experienced the need for temporary healing in a specific situation? What did you do?

3. What calming techniques from chapter 3 can you best use when temporary healing is called for?

4. In the issues of your life where lifelong healing is needed, where are you in that process?

5. Which of the following—faith, endure, time—do you need to better grasp in your healing process?

6. How can you utilize the cognitive triangle to change your thinking, feelings, or behaviors?

Activities

1. Reread the Temporary Healing Worksheet in this chapter and make notes in your journal for a plan when you need to call upon immediate temporary healing in a situation.

2. Write down in your journal the insight or insights you gained in this chapter, and how you can apply them in your life and in your parenting.

Chapter 10

Continuing the Journey

From the time you began this book until now, you have probably begun to see things differently. This may be just the beginning of developing insight for you or it may be a new take on a journey you have been on for years. Perhaps the birthday cake exercise was a new look on boundaries that you hadn't considered before. Or maybe the coping skills of chapter 3 saved you more than once from losing your cool with someone. Maybe you have become intentional in responding rather than reacting to your children.

What have you gleamed so far from these chapters?

The primary goal for you throughout these pages was to help you begin to ask yourself questions that maybe you hadn't asked before. To help you begin to see and understand things a little differently. To encourage you to learn the value of relationships and what is of value in relationships. All these things have helped you to become insightful. You are the insightful parent.

Now, the process doesn't end here. You will continually grow and learn along the way. When your child reaches a new stage and you struggle to control your own feelings in the midst of her teenage puberty, you may remember and re-experience some teenage drama of your own. When your son decides he would rather join drama than the wrestling team, you may feel a bit bewildered that your son is not as interested in athletics as you are. As an insightful parent, you will be able to look at these circumstances and recognize that your reactions are merely your issues, and you can address them accordingly.

In preparing to close this book there are really two areas to consider: you and others. It's that simple.

A successful story of this is a single mother with a child. A few years back the child was suffering from low self-image and poor coping skills. The mother knew enough to bring the child in to counseling. Over a period of time, I saw an improvement in not just the child's symptoms but the mother also. I saw the mother become more confident in her own skin and able to determine which of her child's needs she, as the mother, could meet and which needs the child had to figure out on her own. As a result of working with the girl and her mother over two years, the girl is now making As in school that she never had before and displaying insight and personal control over her emotions. This mother became insightful, and her daughter will continue to reap the rewards of the mother's work.

I appreciated that mother's willingness to grow along with her child. It is a wonderful thing when parents decide that they too want to change for sake of their children and themselves. Parents, we must never put the whole burden on our children to improve. If your children begin counseling, you should also. There are two reasons for this. One, we as parents need to lead by example. Two, if your child is struggling with something, you as a parent are struggling too. As you participate in the journey of healing, whether formally or through personal growth, you'll learn to recognize and appreciate the small steps taken in the process.

It Starts with You

To give back in this world, to be a healthy adult, contributing member of our world, and a parent who helps your children grow, you must take time to be alone. While some scholars may call this selfish, I believe it is the most selfless act you can do on a regular basis. Remember the golden rule: Do unto others what you would have them do unto you. You must first know your value and place in this world before you help your children find their value and place. Do you know your value?

In order to know our value, we must know from where and when we came. We must believe strongly in our inception.

Have you ever stopped to think about creation and our world on a deeper level?

How do you believe life is created? How do you believe the world was created? Before the world began, do you believe you were on the mind of God? Or are you just mere happenstance of a biological fusion? Your answers to these questions form your self-image. They shape how you see yourself and the value you believe you have.

Years ago, I knew a friend who was an only child of a single woman. Single parents have such a burden, and we as a society need to help and not harm their ability to successfully parent. From the cost of living to emotional burdens, to schedules and carpooling, this is quite a difficult job. My friend in particular, his mother was quite stressed, at least I want to believe she was stressed and her frustration was just expressing itself in the wrong ways. One day, we were all sitting in the living room discussing family and the frustrations of their relationship, and she flat out called her son "an accident." Accident—like two cars crashing into each other on the highway. Accident—like spilling milk on the kitchen floor. Accident—like letting the dog run out the front door. She didn't say "surprise" or "unplanned"; she called him an accident in her life.

No matter how planned or unplanned, happy or sad, wealthy or poor your biological parents were when you were conceived: you are not an accident. Your biological conception was only the final step in God's long-term preparation for your birth. Understanding and accepting that your feet are on this earth at the right time for the right reason in the right season is the beginning of insightful parenting. Your inception occurred during the creation of the world and you have always been known by God even if you don't feel known by man. Standing on this foundational truth gives you self-worth and value that reinforces your purpose. Your value and purpose is not dependent on your children, family, or circumstance.

Do you believe you were planned or an accident? Sometimes we toggle between the two, but finding your identity in knowing that before you knew yourself, you were created and known, regardless of what your parents say, can be a very encouraging thought to accept. Regardless of what your parents may say, they were but a small piece in your creation story, and you are no accident.

Journey

My husband, Josh, and I serve on the weekends at a veterans' nursing home. We sing songs and share a message of truth and hope to what may appear to be hopeless situations. Josh was preaching just before the Christmas season and said a profound truth to these servicemen and servicewomen: *It is never too late to change your story.* Amid a wheelchair-bound, cognitively impaired, ninety-plus-year-old audience, he said again, "It is never too late to change your story." I wondered what they were thinking. I wondered at some of their excuses: *"It's too late for me." "Change my story to what? I'm stuck here." "I've been this way for too long. I can't change."* No matter the age, no matter our circumstance, our excuses are still the same.

At the nursing home where we serve, there is one man who has decided it is not too late to change his story. About a year ago, he was ill and asked for my husband to come to his bedside. Over the course of several meetings, he told my husband he wasn't sure how long he had and wanted to make his life right before God. As Josh met with him and led him into a relationship with God through Jesus, the man began to express a sense of peace that he hadn't had before. This only began the changes in his life. Before his decision to change he was estranged from many family members and had only a few close connections. Since his change, he has now reached out to friends and family he hadn't spoken to in years. He is reaching out and rebuilding what would have been a lost cause if he hadn't decided to change.

Change is inevitable in life, so we can let it happen to us or we can be insightful and intentional about making the right kind of changes. Remember, life is like a road trip. Get off the interstate often. Change your speed sometimes and make memories over the spicy dishes at tiny diners. Your story from yesterday is part of your journey today, and you get another chance at making it great tomorrow. Take a moment to look back at where you came from. Now, look ahead at where you are going. These roads connect and you are part of them both. Don't let life be an accident. Make it happen and celebrate the journey.

Insight

How are you doing so far? If you feel I have asked too many questions throughout the book, then I have just asked enough. The questions you have learned to ask yourself and conversations you have begun to have will hopefully continue to develop and grow. You will continue to see beauty and flaws in yourself and others and have the ability to choose what you want to do now with what you know.

There is some truth to the cliché "Innocence is bliss." However, it is perhaps better said "Disengagement, denial, arrogance, entitlement is bliss." Because the only way we can remain innocent in this world is if we turn a blind eye. As parents, we can't turn a blind eye. Not to our children's needs, not to our own needs, or to the needs of those around us. We have a responsibility to find healthy solutions for ourselves, our kids, and our community. This is why our own insight into our unresolved issues, biases, and experiences is the first step. When you begin to see yourself for who you are and accept yourself, you can extend that same grace to others.

Calm, Cool, and Collected

Remaining calm in the midst of stress is an integral piece of insightful parenting. Not only does it help you as a parent keep your thoughts collected, but it also models that one can remain calm in spite of a highly emotional situation around them. Remember the analogy of how a firefighter trains for a fire? He starts in the classroom, then moves to a controlled fire before he ever steps foot into a real fire. You see, fire is uncontrollable and unpredictable. It takes patience and persistence to overcome something that doesn't want to be controlled. In our lives we all have situations and circumstances that seem like a fire to us; they seem to consume our emotions and we surrender to its power.

A firefighter knows you can't fight fire with fire and you can never give into it. A fire needs water. Practicing the art of remaining calm, cool, and collected in the midst of your daily stress or around individuals who trigger you will improve your overall health and well-being in life. Just like a firefighter, an insightful parent has to develop personal awareness to know what skills work for them and how often they need to practice them to be effective.

How about you? How are your coping skills? Which ones work for you? How often do you do them? What coping skills work best for you in the midst of crisis? Which one works best for routine self-care?

Relationships

You are never alone. Even in *Cast Away*, the movie, perhaps the most deserted depiction of isolation I can imagine, Tom Hanks's character, Chuck Noland, quickly realized on the island that he needed to remain in relationship. To keep himself from going crazy, he created a friend, Wilson, a volleyball, and the two became friends. Being in relationships is a basic need to our psyche. Without relationships, we will fail to thrive.

Opportunities for relationships are all around you. Do you look for relationships that build you up or tear you down? Perhaps, you don't look for them, but what types of relationships find you? Remember, a relationship goes two ways. So, if it is not working for you, have a conversation, ask a few questions, or just walk away. Authentic relationships are transparent, and if you can't ask questions, is it a healthy relationship? The goal of healthy relationships is to have a mutual respect and value with each party. The expectations in a healthy relationship should not feel burdensome or an obligation, but be accepted with gratitude.

Family

Family is a never an easy topic. There is no magic pill or simple statement to resolve all discord and denial that exists in families. But family can also love, stick together, and pour into your life. Family can be blood or adopted. Just as you are no accident, you are not in your family by accident. Whether for relationships or for learning, insight helps you determine how to respond in an appropriate manner in any given family situation. Without insight, it is difficult to navigate difficult issues within families.

Across our country, juveniles repeat the cycle of bad decisions and incarcerations they learned from their parents. While they often do blame their parents for their actions, they are equally quick to defend their family from verbal attacks from outsiders. The bond that exists among family is usually unbreakable. However, for people who have experienced violations of trust and major crisis within family, the bond may be quite fragile. In fragile family relationships, it is important to first assess your own heart and intentions. Remember to not react in any situation, and seek help from outsiders to help you evaluate if you are having difficulty working through a problem within the family. Remember, just like all other relationships, establish healthy communication, boundaries, and quality times with the loved ones who pour into you and that you want or need to pour into. Making and maintaining healthy family practices isn't selfish; it's insightful.

How are you today on healthy family practices? How are your family relationships? Is there anyone you need to reach out to or draw back from? What can you teach your children and learn from them about the value of a healthy family? Remember, making family decisions first starts with considering what is best for those living within your four walls, then accommodating extended family.

Feelings

There are two types of people: thinkers and feelers. The truth is, no one is all one or the other. A thinker can feel joy or pain, just as a feeler can complete a math problem or walk through a maze. Feelers are those who first process through their feelings; rational thinking to them comes second. The first thing a feeler does is view life through the window of the soul. Remember, it's a two-way window; we can look into our soul or out into the world. The same insights can be gained through the emotions on the pane whether we are looking into our soul or looking into the world around us. Feelings can be a wonderful resource and fuel to enrich relationships. But without proper control they can be consuming and destructive, paralyzing you from moving or making a complete thought.

We develop insight to our feelings and soul needs by processing feelings from a thinker's mindset. Utilizing the thermometer presented in chapter 3, you can learn to identify needs that stem from an emotion, and recognize what a feeling looks like from a step-by-step process. You can gain control of those feelings that may seem out of whack by making them into a math problem of sorts: 1 (when *this* happens) + 2 (I think/believe *that*) = 3 (and I feel _____). Your positive feelings are meant to enhance life, and the negative ones are meant to be recognized, recorded, and processed. If you spend more time in the negative than positive emotions, work to develop a healthier self-care plan, reach out to our support system, and seek professional help to regain control.

How are you handling your feelings lately? What feelings are you experiencing most? What is the condition of your soul as you look through your soul's window? Is there any feeling you need to process?

Hope

Few things in life can be appreciated or grow without hope. Hope helps us survive the ups and downs of life. Hope is the magnetic force that keeps us on the track of life's rollercoaster. Hope never fails, and never gives up. When we feel we have lost hope, we have simply let it go; hope never loses its value. We know that hope is essential to parenthood because it is the promise we hold to, believing that all our efforts as parents will one day pay off, whether or not we see the results. As an insightful parent you have the ability to find hope for your own life and can then pass on the legacy for your children to find hope in spite of what life brings them.

Consider how closely hope and resilience are related. Resilience is the ability to bounce back and overcome adversity. Therefore, resilience is the ability to find hope regardless of what our circumstances tell us.

How has hope helped you in life? Have you been able to use hope as a resource to help you in insightful parenting? What might be missing for you to have the hope you need to be an insightful parent? To be a healthier individual?

Love

The twin sister to hope: love. Love is the lifeblood of so much of our existence. Love is both a feeling and an action, and like hope, it is a noun and verb. Love motivates us to do the things that bring us joy. Because it is a choice, love holds families together and keeps memories strong of the loved ones who have gone before us. Love is the strongest power in this world. It has the power to forgive and it can heal. Love changes things and love limits things. Boundaries and self-worth exist in love.

It is important to remember we can only give what we already have. You must first love yourself and know your value before you can truly give love to someone else. While it is possible to love others without fully loving ourselves, this will carry us to a point of exhaustion. We have to be willing to act out of love and give ourselves grace when we fall short. Remember the value in your self-care plan and take time to ensure you are healthy and well so that you can give love to your children and family. An insightful parent loves regardless of, not because of, how they feel toward their children. Love is what guides you to the questions: "Is this going to help or harm my child?" "Is this about me or about them?" "Am I going to react or respond in a situation?"

Love is also a filter through which we receive actions. When we have filter of love on the window of our souls, we are less offended by the actions of others. We no longer let the actions of others get under our skin when we are confident and know that we are loved and valued. Genuine, healthy love not only forgives but also takes responsibility when necessary. Love guides us to take responsibility for our own actions, and also against injustices happening around us. Love does not assume burdens it cannot carry but knows at times it must carry the burden of others. Like the single mother who needs a month's rent paid, or the elderly neighbor who needs a hot meal every night, look for the needs around you and help where you can. Love takes action.

Healing

Healing is the process of all of this coming together. Journey. Insight. Coping skills. Relationships. Family. Feelings. Hope. Love. We were created by a process. Plants grow through a process. And champions are made because of the process they endure. Healing is a process, a journey. While we know we are working toward a goal, the goal may change or we may never reach it. But because we might not reach a goal does not mean we give up. When a cancer patient accepts treatment, they know the outcome may still be death, but they know it will extend their time with loved ones. Their healing was not the end result on this earth, but it brought them extended time to be with the ones they loved. Their physical healing happened in the next life, but relational, emotional healing occurred in this life.

Remember faith, endure, and time are what helped me heal. By finding your peace and knowing your purpose you will be inspired to heal not in spite of, but because of what you are and what you have survived. Your life is not an accident and neither is it happenstance. Healing is knowing that you are on a course to a better place and taking the right stops along the way.

What are your stops along the journey of healing? Forgiveness? Love? Acceptance? Peace? Purpose?

The Insightful Parent

I love the ability to view life through the eyes of an insightful parent. You know the value of time and attention. You check your own feelings before you respond to the feeling of your child. You make decisions because they are best for you and your family not because it's trending in your peer group. As an insightful parent, you trust in and hold value in the process of parenting and accept that the results of your hard work may be delayed, yet you have faith that your good work always takes root in your children's lives. While there is so much more about insightful parenting than contained in this book, I believe you have achieved your goal. You have taken the first steps or additional steps toward the journey of insight.

I first sought to teach parents to heal their inner child within so that they do not hurt their children because of their own unresolved hurts. This book has given you tools to begin the work of healing within yourself and also to help your children develop skills of resilience. You can continue this process by asking yourself questions on a daily basis, continuing to educate yourself about how to heal in specific areas of need, and seek help along the way. There is always great value in wise counsel and professional counseling to help you along the journey.

I have one last note to share. The quietest place in my home is my bathroom. In this room, I have placed a prayer that I have memorized and recite almost daily. It is a prayer that you too can join me in making a positive difference in the lives of those we are in relationship with.

"Lord, thank you for the opportunity of allowing
me to help (insert family member names)
become who you have designed them to be. My
role as (wife, mother, father, husband, etc.),
steward of your gift, can either help or harm the
process. Let me help today. This is a much more
peaceful order than trying to be you in their
lives. Amen."

When I started this book, I had one goal: to help each person who reads it grow in insight. You have the basic tools to self-reflect, recognize, and reposition yourself to be a healthy parent. You may want from time to time to revisit the questions at the end of each chapter and even repeat the exercises. We are all on the journey and continue to learn new insights every day. Our daily environments and our children are amazing instruments of instruction if we allow them to be. I have been challenged in the process of completing this book, and I hope you have been challenged in the process of reading it.

Thank you for allowing me to travel this journey with you. There is no clear end to this book because this is only the beginning of insight for many readers. My purpose was to start something in every parent that will help them heal so children don't have to hurt. Can you see how your journey so far has begun the healing process? Can you see how a healed, healthy parent can minimize the hurt in their child's life? When we are healthy we are then ready to parent based on our children's needs, not our own unresolved issues. Please continue the journey. You are worth it. Your children are worth it. And your children's children are worth it.

Appendix A
Paint Cans

Use these cans to *label and identify* thoughts, feelings, or memories that plague you. You are labeling and *separating* these things so they have a place to be *contained* and you can work on them one by one.

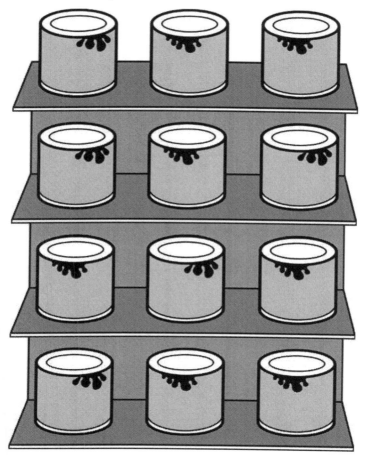

Appendix B
Am Safe vs. Feel Safe

Being safe and feeling safe are two different things. "Am safe" is about the actual *fact* of being safe. Being safe is about people, places, and things that pose *no* imminent risk to us. The risk can be a physical, mental, or emotional threat. But if there is no imminent threat, you *are* safe.

"Feel safe" is about the feeling of being safe. This is not rooted in fact but feeling. Depending on past experience, "feel safe" may tend to be positive or negative toward life. We may feel safe in a rocking chair if we have good memories of them. Conversely, we may not feel safe in a car because we have been in an accident before. How our mind associates a *similar* thing as being the *same* thing from our past is how this "feel safe" can get confused. Although we are safe in the car, we do not feel safe because we are still connecting being in the car now (present) with being in an accident (past).

"Feel safe" is only a problem when it does not line up with "am safe." In short, if we do not feel safe, we tend to think we are not safe. If these beliefs are distorted and are affecting our lives, we have to divide and correct the false beliefs between "'am safe" and "feel safe."

Beside the items listed below write "am safe," "feel safe," "both," or "neither," depending on how it applies to you. Answer honestly.

Your spouse

Your children

Your parents

Your siblings

Grandparents

Home

Work

Place of Worship

Grocery Store

Out in Public

Fill in any additional items:

Appendix C

Your Birthday Cake

Using the description of the Birthday Cake found in Chapter Four to identify the different people in your life. Consider healthy boundaries and relationships, then fill in your tiers on the diagram below, listing those who are in the three various relationship levels in your life. Evaluate which ones might need to move up or down in your tiers and why.

Appendix D
Feelings List

Often, we use a limited list of words to describe how we may feel, or a certain emotion that we may be dealing with. Utilize the list below to find more specific, descriptive words to further define your emotion. This will lead to greater understanding of your emotions and help you get to the root of what they may mean in a specific circumstance.

POSITIVE

OPEN	HAPPY	ALIVE	GOOD
understanding	great	playful	Calm
confident	gay	courageous	Peaceful
reliable	joyous	energetic	at ease
easy	lucky	liberated	comfortable
amazed	fortunate	optimistic	pleased
free	delighted	provocative	encouraged
sympathetic	overjoyed	impulsive	clever
interested	gleeful	free	surprised
satisfied	thankful	frisky	content
receptive	important	animated	quiet
accepting	festive	spirited	certain
kind	ecstatic	thrilled	relaxed
	satisfied	wonderful	serene
	glad		free and easy
	cheerful		bright
	sunny		blessed
	merry		reassured
	elated		
	jubilant		

LOVE	INTERESTED	POSITIVE	STRONG
loving	concerned	eager	impulsive
considerate	affected	keen	free
affectionate	fascinated	earnest	sure
sensitive	intrigued	intent	certain
tender	absorbed	anxious	rebellious
devoted	inquisitive	inspired	unique
attracted	nosy	determined	dynamic
passionate	snoopy	excited	tenacious
admiration	engrossed	enthusiastic	hardy
warm	curious	bold	secure
touched		brave	
sympathy		daring	
close		challenged	
loved		optimistic	
comforted		re-enforced	
drawn toward		confident	
		hopeful	

NEGATIVE

ANGRY	DEPRESSED	CONFUSED	HELPLESS
irritated	lousy	upset	incapable
enraged	disappointed	doubtful	alone
hostile	discouraged	uncertain	paralyzed
insulting	ashamed	indecisive	fatigued
sore	powerless	perplexed	useless
annoyed	diminished	embarrassed	inferior
upset	guilty	hesitant	vulnerable
hateful	dissatisfied	shy	empty
unpleasant	miserable	stupefied	forced
offensive	detestable	disillusioned	hesitant
bitter	repugnant	unbelieving	despair
aggressive	despicable	skeptical	frustrated
resentful	disgusting	distrustful	distressed
inflamed	abominable	misgiving	woeful
provoked	terrible	lost	pathetic
incensed	in despair	unsure	tragic
infuriated	sulky	uneasy	in a stew
cross	bad	pessimistic	dominated
worked up	a sense of loss	tense	
boiling			
fuming			
indignant			

INDIFFERENT	AFRAID	HURT	SAD
Insensitive	fearful	crushed	tearful
Dull	terrified	tormented	sorrowful
Nonchalant	suspicious	deprived	pained
Neutral	anxious	pained	grief
Reserved	alarmed	tortured	anguish
Weary	panic	dejected	desolate
Bored	nervous	rejected	desperate
Preoccupied	scared	injured	pessimistic
Cold	worried	offended	unhappy
disinterested	frightened	afflicted	lonely
Lifeless	timid	aching	grieved
	shaky	victimized	mournful
	restless	heartbroken	dismayed
	doubtful	agonized	
	threatened	appalled	
	cowardly	humiliated	
	quaking	wronged	
	menaced	alienated	
	wary		

Appendix E

Feelings Thermometer

Choose a negative emotion that you deal with and write it in the top banner. Use the space to the right of the thermometer to describe how you feel when you're at a 0 (no negative emotion) and then at a 10 (total presence of the emotion). Then fill in the steps 2 through 9 that occur, and what happens to your thoughts, feelings, actions, as you progress from 0 to 10. This will give you reference points when the emotion next arises.

Notes

1. Erik Erikson, "Psychosocial Stages," accessed September 1, 2017, http://www.simplypsychology.org/Erik-Erikson.html.

2. Abraham Maslow, "Hierarchy of Needs," accessed September 1, 2017, http://www.simplypsychology.org/Maslow.html.

3. Reinhold Neibuhr, "Serenity Prayer," accessed September 1, 2017, prayerfoundation.org/dailyoffice/serenity_prayer_full_version.htm.

4. Romans 8:28, NIV.

5. C. S. Lewis, *The Four Loves* (New York: Harcourt, Brace, 1960).

6. Gary Chapman, *The Five Love Languages: The Secret to Love That Lasts* (Chicago: Northfield Publishing, 2015).

7. First Corinthians 13:4–8, NIV.

8. Brennan Manning, *Abba's Child: The Cry of the Heart for Intimate Belonging*, rev. ed. (Colorado Springs: NavPress, 2015).

9. Dr. Henry Cloud, *Changes That Heal: The Four Changes That Make Everything Better . . . and That Anyone Can Do*, rev. ed. (Grand Rapids, MI: Zondervan, 1993).

About the Author

As a child, Amanda was passionate, energetic, and driven. As a mother, wife, daughter, and friend, she is still all of these. She has been married to the most important man in the world since 2004. They had their first child in 2006, and second in 2010. Between childhood, in-laws, and having a family of her own, Amanda has experienced the pros and cons of family life. Amanda has worked in social services and with children and families since 2000. She has helped youth overcome the struggles and troubles of life and helped many parents do the same. Amanda is passionate about helping families get healthy and she believes this starts with the parents. Amanda has both a bachelor's and master's degree in social work, has published works in the Library of Congress, and is a licensed clinical social worker. While life hasn't been perfect, Amanda is dedicated to leave this world a better place then how she found it.

Contact the Author

Amanda would love to hear how this process has helped you and what insights you have gained as a result. Please email her and share about the stops you have taken along the journey and the memories you have made with your children. Please email Amanda at amandacorbinlcsw@gmail.com.

Contact the Coach/Editor

Janis Whipple, book coach and editor, is always looking to help authors, new and previously published, achieve and complete their next writing project.

Contact her at janiswhipple@gmail.com.

Made in the USA
Columbia, SC
26 November 2017